Lectionary *Advent 2001 to the eve of Adver*

Church House Publishing

Published by Church House Publishing
Church House
Great Smith Street
London SW1P 3NZ

ISBN 0 7151 2056 5 (small)
0 7151 2054 9 (large)

Authorization

The Calendar and Lectionary for Sundays and Principal Festivals in this publication are authorized pursuant to Canon B 2 of the Canons of the Church of England for use until further resolution of the General Synod of the Church of England. The Weekday Lectionaries are authorized from Advent 2000 until the eve of Advent 2004.

Edited by Jonathan Goodall
Designed and typeset by Omnific
Printed in England by ArklePrint Ltd, Northampton

How to use this book

This booklet gives details of the full range of possibilities envisaged in the liturgical calendar and lectionary of *Common Worship*. Its use as a tool for the preparation of worship will require the making of several choices based first on the general celebration of the Christian year by the Church of England as a whole; second on the customary pattern of calendar in the diocese, parish and place of worship; and third on the pattern of services locally.

The **first column** comprises the Calendar of the Church with the days of the year. All observances that are mandatory are given in **bold** type; optional celebrations and commemorations are in ordinary or *italic* type respectively.

The **second column** comprises (a) the readings and psalms for the Principal Service on Sundays and Principal Feasts, and (b) Holy Communion readings and psalms for Festivals and other days of the week. On the Sundays after Trinity, the Old Testament reading and its psalm are divided into two smaller columns, indicating a choice between a 'continuous' reading week by week, or a reading 'related' to the other readings that day.

The **third column** comprises (a) the Sunday Third Service readings and psalms, and (b) the weekday Office readings: it will probably be most used at Morning Prayer.

The **fourth column** comprises (a) the Sunday Second Service readings and psalms, and (b) the weekday Second Office (with additional material that enables this to be used as an alternative Holy Communion lectionary): it will probably be most used at Evening Prayer.

The **fifth column** comprises psalms used at Morning Prayer (*MP*) and Evening Prayer (*EP*); and also the provision of a psalm for those who regularly pray once a day (Daily Prayer, *DP*). At various times in the calendar (such as between All Saints and Advent) an alternative course of psalms is given on weekdays; either series may be used, but once begun should be followed consistently.

Sundays, Principal Feasts and Holy Days, and Festivals

Three sets of psalms and readings are provided for each Sunday, Principal Holy Days and Festivals.

The **Principal Service Lectionary** is intended for use at the principal service of the day (whether this service is Holy Communion or some other authorized form). In most Church communities, this is likely to be the mid-morning service, but the minister is free to decide which service time normally constitutes the Principal Service of the day. This lectionary may be used twice if required: such as at an early celebration of Holy Communion and then again at a later one.

If only **two readings** are used from the provision for the Principal Service and that service is Holy Communion, the second reading must always be the Gospel reading. When the Principal Service lectionary is used at a service other than Holy Communion, the Gospel reading need not always be chosen.

The **Second Service Lectionary** is intended for a second main service. In many churches, this lectionary may be the appropriate provision for a Sunday afternoon or evening service. A Gospel reading is always provided so that this lectionary can be used where the second main service is a celebration of Holy Communion.

The **Third Service Lectionary**, with shorter readings, is intended where a third set of psalms and readings is needed and is most appropriate for use at an office. A Gospel reading is not always provided, so this lectionary is not suitable for use at Holy Communion.

Weekdays

Three lectionaries are provided, each on a two-year cycle.

The **Holy Communion Lectionary** is for use at weekday celebrations of Holy Communion, normally in places with a daily or near-daily celebration with a regular congregation. It may also be used as an Office Lectionary where brief readings are needed.

The **Office Lectionary** is for use at a daily recitation of the Office especially where there is a regular congregation; the readings are generally in sequence; it will probably be most used at *Morning Prayer*.

The **Second Office Lectionary** is for use at a daily recitation of the office perhaps with an occasional congregation, or an occasional office or time of prayer; the readings, though often related, are generally not in sequence; it will probably be most used at *Evening Prayer*. However, a psalm, and where necessary a Gospel reading, is also supplied to enable its use as an **Alternative Holy Communion Lectionary**, particularly in places where there are only one or two mid-week celebrations.

Psalms

A psalm cycle, often with seasonal emphasis and appropriate repetition, is provided for use at Morning Prayer [*MP*] and Evening Prayer [*EP*]. At certain points in the year an alternative series of psalmody is given. An alternative cycle for the whole year is provided to be recited at a single daily office, here simply called Daily Prayer [*DP*].

A further cycle is provided (*see* page 71) largely replicating the monthly course adopted in the *Book of Common Prayer*.

A limited number of psalms are marked with an asterisk. These are psalms used as invitatory psalms at Morning Prayer, the Night Prayer (Compline) psalms and psalms 58, 83 and 109. Such psalms may be omitted if they are to be used at another service or for pastoral reasons. An asterisk does not however mean that the psalm should be omitted.

Liturgical Colours

Colours are indicated by single letters: the first (upper-case initial) for the season or festival; and occasionally a second (lower-case initial) for an optional celebration on that day. Thus, for example, *Gr* for the celebration of a Lesser Festival for which the liturgical colour is red, in an otherwise 'green' season.

Common of the Saints

General readings and psalms for saints' days can be found on pages 65–68; for some particular celebrations, other readings are suggested there.

Special Occasions

Readings and psalms for special occasions can be found on pages 69–70.

Notes on the Calendar 2 December 2001– 30 November 2002

Sundays

All Sundays celebrate the paschal mystery of the death and resurrection of the Lord. They also reflect the character of the seasons in which they are set.

Principal Feasts

On these days Holy Communion is celebrated in every cathedral and parish church, and this celebration (required by Canon B14) may not be displaced by any other celebration, and may only be dispensed with in accordance with the provision of Canon B14A.

Except in the case of Christmas Day and Easter Day, the celebration of the feast *begins with Evening Prayer on the day before the feast*, and the collect at that Evening Prayer is that of the feast. In the case of Christmas Eve and Easter Eve, there is proper liturgical provision, including a collect, for the whole day.

The Presentation of Christ in the Temple (Candlemas) is celebrated either on Saturday 2 February or Sunday 3 February (thus replacing the provision for the Second Sunday before Lent).

All Saints' Day and **All Saints' Sunday** (1 and 3 November) may both be celebrated, or either may be celebrated.

Because 25 March is the Monday of Holy Week in 2002, the **Annunciation of Our Lord to the Blessed Virgin Mary** is transferred to 8 April.

Other Principal Holy Days

These days, and the liturgical provision for them, may not be displaced by any other celebration.

Ash Wednesday (13 February) and **Maundy Thursday** (28 March) are Principal Holy Days. On both these days Holy Communion is celebrated in every cathedral or parish church, except where there is dispensation under Canon B14A.

Good Friday (29 March) is a Principal Holy Day.

Eastertide

The paschal character of **the Great Fifty Days of Eastertide**, from Easter Day (31 March) to Pentecost (19 May),should be celebrated throughout the season, and should not be displaced by other celebrations. Except for a patronal or dedication festival, no festival may displace the celebration of a Sunday in Eastertide as a memorial of the resurrection, and no saint's day may be celebrated in Easter Week. The paschal character of the season should be retained on those weekdays when saints' days are celebrated.

The three days before Ascension Day (6–8 May), are customarily observed as **Rogation Days**, when prayer is offered for God's blessing on the fruits of the earth and on human labour.

The nine days **after Ascension Day until the eve of Pentecost** (10–18 May) are observed as days of prayer and preparation for the celebration of the outpouring of the Holy Spirit.

Festivals

These days, and the liturgical provision for them, are not usually displaced. For each day there is full liturgical provision for Holy Communion, Morning and Evening Prayer, and an optional so-called First Evening Prayer on the evening before the festival where this is required.

Festivals may *not* be celebrated on Sundays in Advent, Lent or Eastertide, the Baptism of Christ or Christ the King, or weekdays between Palm Sunday and the Second Sunday of Easter. Otherwise, festivals falling on a Sunday may be kept on that day or transferred to the Monday (or, at the discretion of the minister, to the next suitable weekday). Festivals coinciding with a Principal Feast or a Principal Holy Day are transferred to the first available day.

The Thursday after Trinity Sunday (30 May) may be observed as the **Day of Thanksgiving for the Institution of Holy Communion** (sometimes known as *Corpus Christi*), and may be kept as a Festival.

Other Celebrations

Mothering Sunday falls on 10 March, the Fourth Sunday of Lent. Alternative prayers and readings are provided for the Principal Service.

Bible Sunday may be celebrated on 27 October, displacing the Last Sunday after Trinity, and appropriate readings are provided.

Local Celebrations

The celebration of **the patron saint** or **the title of a church** is kept either as a Festival or as a Principal Feast.

The **Dedication Festival** of a church is the anniversary of the date of its dedication or consecration. This is kept either as a Festival or as a Principal Feast.

When kept as Principal Feasts, the Patronal and Dedication Festivals may be transferred to the nearest Sunday, unless that day is already a Principal Feast or one of the following days: the First Sunday of Advent, the Baptism of Christ, the First Sunday of Lent, the Fifth Sunday of Lent, or Palm Sunday.

If the actual date is not known, the Dedication Festival may be celebrated on 6 October (displacing the Nineteenth Sunday after Trinity) or 27 October (displacing the Last Sunday after Trinity). Readings can be found on page 65.

Harvest Thanksgiving may be celebrated on any Sunday in autumn, replacing the provision for that day, provided it does not supersede any Principal Feast or Festival.

Diocesan and other local provision may be made in **the calendar of the saints** to supplement the general calendar, in accordance with Canon B6, paragraph 5.

Lesser Festivals

Lesser Festivals, which are listed in the calendar, are observed in a manner appropriate to a particular place. Each is provided with a collect, psalm and readings, which may supersede the collect of the week and the Daily Eucharistic Lectionary (DEL). For the lectionary details *see* pp.65–68. The weekday psalms and readings at Morning and Evening Prayer are not usually superseded by those for Lesser Festivals, but at the minister's discretion psalms and readings provided on these days for use at Holy Communion may be used instead at Morning or Evening Prayer.

The minister may be selective in the Lesser Festivals that are observed and may also keep some, or all of them, as Commemorations, perhaps especially in Lent where the character of the season ought to be sustained. If the Day of Thanksgiving for the Institution of Holy Communion (30 May) is not kept as a Festival, it may be kept as a Lesser Festival.

When a Lesser Festival falls on a Principal Feast or Holy Day or on a Festival, its celebration is normally omitted for that year, but, where there is sufficient reason, it may, at the discretion of the minister, be celebrated on the nearest available day.

Commemorations

Commemorations, which are listed in the calendar, are made by a mention in prayers of intercession. They are not provided with collect, psalm and readings, and do not replace the usual weekday provision at Holy Communion or at Morning and Evening Prayer.

The minister may be selective in the Commemorations that are made.

Only where there is an established celebration in the wider church or where the day has a special local significance may a Commemoration be observed as a Lesser Festival, with liturgical provision from the common material for holy men and women.

In designating a Commemoration as a Lesser Festival, the minister must remember the need to maintain the spirit of the season, especially of Advent and Lent.

Days of Discipline and Self-Denial

The weekdays of Lent and every Friday in the year are days of discipline and self-denial, with the exception of Principal Feasts, Festivals outside Lent and Fridays from Easter Day to Pentecost. The day preceding a Principal Feast may also be appropriately kept as a day of discipline and self-denial in preparation for the feast.

Ember Days

Ember Days should be kept, under the bishop's directions, in the week before an ordination as days of prayer for those to be ordained deacon or priest.

Ember Days may also be kept even when there is no ordination in the diocese as more general days of prayer for those who serve the Church in its various ministries, both ordained and lay, and for vocations. Traditionally they have been observed on the Wednesday, Friday and Saturday in the week before the Third Sunday of Advent, the Second Sunday of Lent, and the Sundays nearest to 29 June and 29 September.

Ordinary Time

Ordinary Time comprises two periods in the year: the period from the day after the Feast of the Presentation of Christ until the day before Ash Wednesday, and that from the day after the Feast of Pentecost until the day before the First Sunday of Advent.

During Ordinary Time, there is no seasonal emphasis, except that the period between All Saints' Day and the First Sunday of Advent is observed as a time to celebrate and reflect upon the reign of Christ in earth and heaven.

Liturgical Colours

Appropriate liturgical colours are suggested in this booklet: they are not mandatory; traditional or local use may be followed.

Notes on the Lectionary

The Sunday and festal readings for the First Sunday of Advent 2001 to Andrew the Apostle (the eve of Advent) 2002 are from **Year A**, which offers a semi-continuous reading of Matthew's Gospel at the Sunday Principal Service throughout the year. The weekday readings are from **Year Two**.

All **Bible references** (except to the Psalms) are to the *New Revised Standard Version* (New York, 1989). Those who use other Bible translations should check the verse numbers against that version. The references give book, chapter and verse, in that order.

References to the psalms are to the *Common Worship* Psalter, published in *Common Worship: Services and Prayers for the Church of England* (Church House Publishing, London, 2000). A table showing the verse number differences between this and the Psalter published in the *Book of Common Prayer* is provided on the *Common Worship* web site (http://www.cofe.anglican.org/commonworship/)

Where optional additional verses or psalms are set, the references appear in brackets. A simple choice between two alternative readings is indicated by an italicized '*or*' placed between references. For longer psalms, a shorter alternative is sometimes offered, indicated by a reference in brackets.

Where a reading from the **Apocrypha** is offered, an alternative Old Testament reading is provided.

In the choice of **readings other than the Gospel** reading, the minister should ensure that, in any year, a balance is maintained between readings from the Old and New Testaments and that, where a particular biblical book is appointed to be read over several weeks, the choice ensures that the continuity of one book is not lost.

On the Sundays after Trinity, the Principal Service Lectionary provides **alternative Old Testament readings and psalms**. References in the right-hand column (under the heading 'Related') *relate* the Old Testament reading and the psalm to the Gospel reading. Those in the left-hand column (under the heading 'Continuous') offer a *semi-continuous* reading of Old Testament texts where the Old Testament reading and its complementary psalm stand independently of the other readings. One column should be followed for the whole sequence of Sundays after Trinity.

Notes on Collects

The collects and post communions for Sundays, Principal Feasts and Holy Days, and Festivals may be found in *Common Worship: Services and Prayers for the Church of England* (pp.375–523). All the *Common Worship* collects and post communions, including those for Lesser Festivals, the Common of the Saints, and Special Occasions, are published in both the president's edition of *Common Worship*, and in *The Christian Year: collects and post communions for Sundays and festivals* (Church House Publishing, London, 1997).

Where a collect ends 'through Jesus Christ ... now and for ever' the minister may omit the longer trinitarian ending and use the shorter ending, 'through Jesus Christ our Lord', to which the people respond 'Amen'. The longer ending, however, is to be preferred at a service of Holy Communion.

The collect for each Sunday is used at Evening Prayer on the Saturday preceding, except where that Saturday is a Principal Feast, or a Festival, or the eve of Christmas Day or Easter Day. The collect for each Sunday is also used on the weekdays following, except where other provision is made.

Abbreviations used in this book

Alt	Alternative
Bp	Bishop
BVM	Blessed Virgin Mary
Cant	Canticle
Comps	Companions
DEL Week	Daily Eucharistic Lectionary
DP	Daily Prayer – Single Office Psalmody
EP	Evening Prayer
G	Green
HC	Holy Communion: *used where additional references are given to provide alternative texts for use at a celebration of Holy Communion (most often the provision of a psalm or gospel)*
Mm	Martyrs
MP	Morning Prayer
P or p	Purple or Violet
P(La)	Purple or Lent Array
Ps & Pss	Psalmody
R or r	Red
Ss	Saints
vv	Verses: used where the source is not subdivided into chapters
W or w	White (Gold is indicated where its use would be appropriate)
Eccles	Ecclesiastes
Ecclus	Ecclesiasticus
Sol	Song of Solomon (also called Song of Songs)

Standard abbreviations have been used for other books of the Bible where necessary.

Alternative dates

The following may be celebrated on the alternative dates indicated:

Chad
– with Cedd on 26 October instead of 2 March
Cuthbert – on 4 September instead of 20 March
Matthias the Apostle
– on 24 February instead of 14 May
The Visit of the Blessed Virgin Mary to Elizabeth
– on 2 July instead of 31 May
Thomas the Apostle
– on 31 December instead of 3 July
The Blessed Virgin Mary
– on 8 September instead of 15 August
Thomas Becket
– on 7 July instead of 29 December

If any of the four festivals is celebrated on the alternative date, these provisions should be followed:

Holy Communion	Office	2nd Office or Alt HC	Psalmody
If Matthias the Apostle is celebrated on 25 February (transferred from 24 February, the Second Sunday in Lent), the following provision is used for 14 May:			
Acts 20.17–27	1 Samuel 16.1–13*a*	Exodus 11	*MP* 66, 149
Psalm 68.9–10, 18–19	1 John 3.19–end	2 Timothy 1.8–18	*EP* 120, 121, 133
John 17.1–11		*HC Ps 35.23–26; Luke 6.39–end*	*DP* 122, 123
		**or 1 Sam 10.1–10; 1 Cor 12.1–13*	
		(Alternative readings in preparation for Pentecost)	
If the Visit of the Blessed Virgin Mary to Elizabeth is celebrated on 2 July, the following provision is used for 31 May:			
1 Peter 4.7–13	Proverbs 23.19—24.2	Ecclesiastes 11	*MP* 13, 14
Psalm 96.10–end	Luke 16.1–9	Colossians 3.1–11	*EP* 15, 16
Mark 11.11–25 [26]		*HC Ps 128; Mark 13.24–end*	*DP* 22
If Thomas the Apostle is celebrated on 21 December, the following provision is used for 3 July:			
Amos 5.14–15, 21–24	Numbers 22.41—23.12	Job 17	*MP* 84
Psalm 50.7–14	Luke 22.63–end	John 11.1–16	*EP* [85] 86
Matthew 8.28–end		*HC Ps 6.1–5*	*DP* 51
If the Blessed Virgin Mary is celebrated on Sunday 8 September (or 9 September, transferred from 8 September) the following provision is used for 15 August:			
Ezekiel 12.1–12	Judges 14	1 Chronicles 29.1–9	*MP* 25
Psalm 78.58–64	Romans 12.9–end	1 Corinthians 4	*EP* 26, 27
Matthew 18.21—19.1		*HC Ps 123; Luke 9.1–17*	*DP* 87

Key to the tables

Sundays (and Principal Feasts, other Principal Holy Days, and Festivals)

		Principal Service	3rd Service	2nd Service	Psalmody
Day	**Date** *Colour* **Sunday** / **Feast**† / Festival††	Main Service of the day: Holy Communion, Morning Prayer, Evening Prayer, or A Service of the Word.	Shorter Readings, an Office lectionary, probably used at Morning Prayer where Holy Communion is the Principal Service.	2nd main Service, probably used at Evening Prayer; adaptable for Holy Communion.	Daily Prayer, single office

Weekdays

		Holy Communion	Office	2nd Office or Alt HC	Psalmody
Day	**Date** *Colour* Lesser Festival* [optional] *Commemoration* [optional]	Weekday readings	Probably used at Morning Prayer.	Probably used at Evening Prayer.	Morning Prayer Evening Prayer Daily Prayer

† Principal Feasts and other Principal Holy Days are printed in **bold**.
†† Festivals are printed in roman typeface.
* The ascriptions given to holy men and women in the Calendar (such as martyr, teacher of the faith, etc.) have often had to be abbreviated in this almanac for want of space; the particular ascription given is there to be helpful if needing to choose Collects and readings from Common of the Saints; where several ascriptions are used (e.g. bishop & martyr), traditionally the last ascription given is the most important and therefore the guiding one.

		Principal Service	3rd Service	2nd Service	Psalmody
Sunday	**2 December** *P* **1st Sunday of Advent**	Isaiah 2.1–5 Psalm 122 Romans 13.11–end Matthew 24.36–44	Psalm 44 Micah 4.1–7 1 Thessalonians 5.1–11	Psalm 9 [*or* 9.1–8] Isaiah 52.1–12 Matthew 24.15–28	*DP* 80

		Holy Communion	Office	2nd Office or Alt HC	Psalmody
Monday	**3 December** *P* *Francis Xavier, missionary*	Isaiah 4.2–6 Psalm 122 Matthew 8.5–11	Amos 1.1,13—end of 2 Matthew 21.1–11	Genesis 1.1–19 Philippians 1.1–14 *HC Ps 104.1–6; Mark 1.1–8*	*MP* 70,75 *EP* 94 *DP* 70
Tuesday	**4 December** *P* *John of Damascus, monk, teacher of the faith; Nicholas Ferrar, deacon*	Isaiah 11.1–10 Psalm 72.1–4,18–end Luke 10.21–24	Amos 3.1–11 Matthew 21.12–22	Genesis 1.20—2.3 Philippians 1.15–end *HC Ps 8.4–end; Mark 1.9–13*	*MP* 50 *EP* 144 *DP* 50
Wednesday	**5 December** *P*	Isaiah 25.6–10*a* Psalm 23 Matthew 15.29–37	Amos 3.12—4.5 Matthew 21.23–32	Genesis 2.4–17 Philippians 2.1–11 *HC Ps 33.4–9; Mark 1.14–28*	*MP* 28,76 *EP* 44 *DP* 23
Thursday	**6 December** *Pw* Nicholas, bishop (see p.67)	Isaiah 26.1–6 Psalm 118.18–27*a* Matthew 7.21, 24–27	Amos 4.6–end Matthew 21.33–end	Genesis 2.18–end Philippians 2.12–18 *HC Ps 34.11–16; Mark 1.29–34*	*MP* 62,82 *EP* 11,12 *DP* 118
Friday	**7 December** *Pw* Ambrose, bishop, teacher of the faith (see p.66)	Isaiah 29.17–end Psalm 27.1–4, 16–17 Matthew 9.27–31	Amos 5.1–17 Matthew 22.1–14	Genesis 3.1–19 Philippians 3.1, 7–16 *HC Ps 53; Mark 1.35–end*	*MP* 40 *EP* 42, 43 *DP* 27
Saturday	**8 December** *Pw* Conception of the Blessed Virgin Mary (see p.65)	Isaiah 30.19–21, 23–26 Psalm 146.4–end Matthew 9.35—10.1, 6–8	Amos 5.18–end Matthew 22.15–22	Genesis 3.20–end Philippians 3.17—4.1 *HC Ps 32.9–end; Mark 2.1–12*	*MP* 9 *EP* 123, 130 *DP* 147

		Principal Service	3rd Service	2nd Service	Psalmody
Sunday	**9 December** *P* **2nd Sunday of Advent**	Isaiah 11.1–10 Psalm 72.1–7, 18–19 [*or* 72.1–7] Romans 15.4–13 Matthew 3.1–12	Psalm 80 Amos 7 Luke 1.5–20	Psalms 11 [28] 1 Kings 18.17–39 John 1.19–28	*DP* 72
		Holy Communion	**Office**	**2nd Office or Alt HC**	**Psalmody**
Monday	**10 December** *P*	Isaiah 35 Psalm 85.7–end Luke 5.17–26	Amos 6 Matthew 22.23–33	Genesis 4.1–16 Philippians 4.4–9 *HC Ps 142.5–7; Mark 2.13–17*	*MP* 70 [75] *EP* 94 *DP* 85
Tuesday	**11 December** *P*	Isaiah 40.1–11 Psalm 96.1, 10–end Matthew 18.12–14	Amos 7 Matthew 22.34–end	Genesis 6 1 Thessalonians 1 *HC Ps 25.15–20; Mark 2.18–22*	*MP* 50 *EP* 144 *DP* 96
Wednesday	**12 December** *P* Ember Day (see p.6)	Isaiah 40.25–end Psalm 103.8–13 Matthew 11.28–end	Amos 8 Matthew 23.1–12	Genesis 7 1 Thessalonians 2.1–12 *HC Ps 93; Mark 2.23–end*	*MP* 28, 76 *EP* 44 *DP* 103
Thursday	**13 December** *Pr* Lucy, martyr (see p.65) *Samuel Johnson, moralist*	Isaiah 41.13–20 Psalm 145.1, 8–13 Matthew 11.11–15	Amos 9 Matthew 23.13–26	Genesis 8.1–12 1 Thessalonians 2.13–end *HC Ps 95.1–5; Mark 3.1–6*	*MP* 62, 82 *EP* 11, 12 *DP* 145
Friday	**14 December** *Pw* John of the Cross, poet, teacher of the faith (see p.66) Ember Day	Isaiah 48.17–19 Psalm 1 Matthew 11.16–19	Haggai 1 Matthew 23.27–end	Genesis 8.13–end 1 Thessalonians 3 *HC Ps 65.8–end; Mark 3.7–12*	*MP* 40 *EP* 42, 43 *DP* 1
Saturday	**15 December** *P* Ember Day	Ecclesiasticus 48.1–4, 9–11 *or* 2 Kings 2.9–12 Psalm 80.1–4, 18–19 Matthew 17.10–13	Haggai 2.1–9 Matthew 24.1–14	Genesis 9.8–19 1 Thessalonians 4.1–12 *HC Ps 65.4–7; Mark 3.13–19*	*MP* 9 *EP* 123, 130 *DP* 9

		Principal Service	3rd Service	2nd Service	Psalmody
Sunday	**16 December** *P* **3rd Sunday of Advent**	Isaiah 35 Psalm 146.4–end *or Canticle:* Magnificat James 5.7–10 Matthew 11.2–11	Psalm 68.1–19 Zephaniah 3.14–end Philippians 4.4–7	Psalms 12 [14] Isaiah 5.8–end Acts 13.13–41 *HC John 5.31–40*	*DP* 146

		Holy Communion	Office	2nd Office or Alt HC	Psalmody
From 17 December to the Eve of the Baptism of Christ, the Second Office lectionary may not be used as an alternative eucharistic lectionary.					
Monday	**17 December** *P* *Eglantine Jebb, social reformer* *O Sapientia*	Genesis 49.2, 8–10 Psalm 72.1–5, 18–end Matthew 1.1–17	Daniel 9.15–19 Philippians 4.4–8	Ecclesiasticus 24.1–9 *or* Proverbs 8.1–11 1 Corinthians 2.1–13	*MP* 113 *EP* 90, 111 *DP* 121, 122
Tuesday	**18 December** *P*	Jeremiah 23.5–8 Psalm 72.1, 6–8, 18–end Matthew 1.18–24	Genesis 3.8–15 Revelation 12.1–10	Exodus 3.1–6 Acts 7.20–36	*MP* 114 *EP* 106 *DP* 123, 124
Wednesday	**19 December** *P*	Judges 13.2–7, 24–end Psalm 71.3–8 Luke 1.5–25	Isaiah 11.1–10 Titus 1.1–16	Song of Songs 2.8–14 Romans 15.7–13	*MP* 115 *EP* 50 *DP* 125, 126
Thursday	**20 December** *P*	Isaiah 7.10–14 Psalm 24.1–6 Luke 1.26–38	1 Samuel 2.1*b*–10 Titus 2.1–10	Isaiah 22.20–23 Revelation 3.7–13	*MP* 116.1–8 *EP* 89.1–34 *DP* 127, 128
Friday	**21 December** *P*	Zephaniah 3.14–18 Psalm 33.1–4, 11–12, 20–end Luke 1.39–45	2 Samuel 7.1–17 Titus 2.11—3.8*a*	Numbers 24.15*b*–19 Revelation 22.10–21	*MP* 116.9–end *EP* 27 *DP* 129, 130
Saturday	**22 December** *P*	1 Samuel 1.24–end Psalm 113 Luke 1.46–56	2 Samuel 7.18–end Galatians 3.1–14	Jeremiah 30.7–11*a* Acts 4.1–12	*MP* 146, 147 *EP* 118 *DP* 131, 133

		Principal Service	3rd Service	2nd Service	Psalmody
Sunday	**23 December** *P* **4th Sunday of Advent**	Isaiah 7.10–16 Psalm 80.1–8, 18–20 [*or* 80.1–8] Romans 1.1–7 Matthew 1.18–end	Psalm 144 Micah 5.2–5*a* Luke 1.26–38	Psalms 113 [126] 1 Samuel 1.1–20 Revelation 22.6–end *HC Luke 1.39–45*	*DP* 132
		If Advent antiphons are being used, EP: Psalm 80; Isaiah 7.10–15; Matthew 1.18–23			
		Holy Communion	Morning Prayer	Evening Prayer	Psalmody
Monday	**24 December** *P* **Christmas Eve**	*only used on 24th morning:* 2 Samuel 7.1–5, 8–11, 16 Psalm 89.2, 19–27 Acts 13.16–26 Luke 1.67–79	Baruch 4.36—5.9 *or* Isaiah 59.15*b*–end Galatians 3.23—4.7	Zechariah 2 Revelation 1.1–8	*MP* 45, 46 *EP* 85 *DP* 89.1–37
Tuesday	**25 December** *Gold or W* Christmas Day	*Any of the following three sets of Principal Service readings may be used on the evening of Christmas Eve and on Christmas Day. Set III should be used at some point during the celebration.*			

Principal Service Set I	Set II	Set III	3rd Service	2nd Service	Psalmody
Isaiah 9.2–7 Psalm 96 Titus 2.11–14 Luke 2.1–14 [15–20]	Isaiah 62.6–end Psalm 97 Titus 3.4–7 Luke 2.[1–7] 8–20	Isaiah 52.7–10 Psalm 98 Hebrews 1.1–4 [5–12] John 1.1–14	Isaiah 62.1–5 Matthew 1.18–25	Isaiah 65.17–end Philippians 2.5–11 *or* Luke 2.1–20 *if it has not been used at the Principal Service*	*MP* 110, 117 *EP* 8 *DP* 8

		Principal Service	3rd Service	2nd Service	Psalmody
Wednesday	**26 December** *R* Stephen, deacon, martyr	2 Chronicles 24.20–22 *or* Acts 7.51–end Psalm 119.161–168 Acts 7.51–end *or* Galatians 2.16*b*–20 Matthew 10.17–22	Jeremiah 26.12–15 Acts 6	Genesis 4.1–10 Matthew 23.34–end	*MP* 13, 31.1–8, 150 *EP* 57, 86 *DP* 57
Thursday	**27 December** *W* John, apostle and evangelist	Exodus 33.7–11*a* Psalm 117 1 John 1 John 21.19*b*–end	Exodus 33.12–end 1 John 2.1–11	Isaiah 6.1–8 1 John 5.1–12	*MP* 21, 147.13–end *EP* 97 *DP* 97
Friday	**28 December** *R* The Holy Innocents	Jeremiah 31.15–17 Psalm 124 1 Corinthians 1.26–29 Matthew 2.13–18	Baruch 4.21–27 *or* Genesis 37.13–20 Matthew 18.1–10	Isaiah 49.14–25 Mark 10.13–16	*MP* 36, 146 *EP* 123, 128 *DP* 123
Saturday	**29 December** *Wr* Thomas Becket, archbishop, martyr (see p.65)	1 John 2.3–11 Psalm 96.1–4 Luke 2.22–35	2 Samuel 23.13–17*b* 2 John	Isaiah 12 John 2.1–11	*MP* 20, 149 *EP* 61, 99 *DP* 20

		Principal Service	3rd Service	2nd Service	Psalmody
Sunday	**30 December** W **1st Sunday of Christmas**	Isaiah 63.7–9 Psalm 148 [*or* 148.7–14] Hebrews 2.10–end Matthew 2.13–end	Psalm 105.1–11 Isaiah 35.1–6 Galatians 3.23–end	Psalm 132 Isaiah 49.7–13 Philippians 2.1–11 *HC Luke 2.41–end*	*DP* 45

		Holy Communion	Office	2nd Office or Alt HC	Psalmody
Monday	**31 December** W *John Wyclif, reformer*	1 John 2.18–21 Psalm 96.1, 11–end John 1.1–18	1 Kings 3.5–14 James 4.13—5.11 *or:* 1st EP of Naming and Circumcision of Jesus: Psalm 148; Jeremiah 23.1–6; Colossians 2.8–15	Isaiah 65.16–25 Revelation 21.1–6	*MP* 132, 117 *EP* 148 *DP* 114, 117
Tuesday	**1 January** W Naming and Circumcision of Jesus	Numbers 6.22–end Psalm 8 Galatians 4.4–7 Luke 2.15–21	Genesis 17.1–13 Romans 2.17–end	Deuteronomy 30.[1–10] 11–end Acts 3.1–16	*MP* 103, 150 *EP* 115 *DP* 150
Wednesday	**2 January** W Basil the Great and Gregory of Nazianzus, bishops, teachers of the faith (see p.66) *Seraphim, monk, spiritual guide; Vedanayagam Samuel Azariah, bishop, evangelist*	1 John 2.22–28 Psalm 98.1–4 John 1.19–28	1 Kings 19.1–8 Ephesians 4.1–16	Genesis 12.1–7 John 6.1–14	*MP* 89.5–18, 146 *EP* 66 *DP* 66
Thursday	**3 January** W	1 John 2.29—3.6 Psalm 98.2–7 John 1.29–34	1 Kings 19.9–18 Ephesians 4.17–end	Genesis 28.10–end John 6.15–27	*MP* 111, 147.1–12 *EP* 46, 48 *DP* 111
Friday	**4 January** W	1 John 3.7–10 Psalm 98.1, 8–end John 1.35–42	Joshua 3.14—4.7 Ephesians 5.1–20	Exodus 3.1–12 John 9.1–12, 35–38	*MP* 112, 148 *EP* 89.1–4, 19–29 *DP* 112
Saturday	**5 January** W	1 John 3.11–21 Psalm 100 John 1.43–end	Jonah 2.2–9 Ephesians 6.10–20 **1st EP of Epiphany:** Isaiah 49.1–13; John 4.7–26	Isaiah 49.1–13 John 4.7–26	*MP* 113, 149 *EP* 96, 97 *DP* 100

			Principal Service	3rd Service	2nd Service	Psalmody
Sunday	**6 January** Epiphany	*Gold or W*	Isaiah 60.1–6 Psalm 72.[1–9] 10–15 Ephesians 3.1–12 Matthew 2.1–12	Jeremiah 31.7–14 John 1.29–34	Baruch 4.36—end of 5 *or* Isaiah 60.1–9 John 2.1–11	*MP* 132, 113 *EP* 98, 100 *DP* 98
Monday	**7 January** Baptism of Christ	*Gold or W*	Isaiah 42.1–9 Psalm 29 Acts 10.34–43 Matthew 3.13–end	Psalm 89.19–29 Exodus 14.15–22 1 John 5.6–9	Psalms 46, 47 Joshua 3.1–8, 14–end Hebrews 1.1–12 *HC Luke 3.15–22*	*DP* 29
			Holy Communion	**Office**	**2nd Office or Alt HC**	**Psalmody**
Tuesday	**8 January** DEL week 1	W	1 Samuel 1.9–20 *Canticle:* 1 Samuel 2.1, 4–8 *or* Magnificat Mark 1.21–28	Genesis 2.4–end Luke 3.15–22	1 Kings 3.1–15 Romans 1.18–end *HC Ps 119.33–40; Mark 4.33–34*	*MP* 97, 146 *EP* 145 *DP* 8
Wednesday	**9 January**	W	1 Samuel 3.1–10, 19–20 Psalm 40.1–4, 7–10 Mark 1.29–39	Genesis 3 Luke 4.1–13	1 Kings 3.16–end Romans 2.1–16 *HC Ps 72.12–15; Mark 4.35–end*	*MP* 66, 147.13–end *EP* 81 *DP* 105
Thursday	**10 January** *William Laud, archbishop*	W	1 Samuel 4.1–11 Psalm 44.10–15, 24–25 Mark 1.40–end	Genesis 4 Luke 4.14–30	1 Kings 4.29–end Romans 3.1–20 *HC Ps 72.16–19; Mark 5.1–20*	*MP* 24, 148 *EP* 72, 98 *DP* 95
Friday	**11 January** *Mary Slessor, missionary*	W	1 Samuel 8.4–7, 10–end Psalm 89.15–18 Mark 2.1–12	Genesis 6.1–8 Luke 4.31–37	1 Kings 5.1–12 Romans 3.21–end *HC Ps 133; Mark 5.21–end*	*MP* 57, 147.1–12 *EP* 36, 46 *DP* 57
Saturday	**12 January** Aelred, abbot (see p.67) *Benedict Biscop, abbot*	W	1 Samuel 9.1–4, 17–19; 10.1 Psalm 21.1–6 Mark 2.13–17	Genesis 6.9–end Luke 4.38–44	1 Kings 6.1–13 Romans 4 *HC Ps 89.20–29; Mark 6.1–6a*	*MP* 21, 149 *EP* 8, 20 *DP* 20

			Principal Service	3rd Service	2nd Service	Psalmody
Sunday	**13 January** **2nd Sunday of Epiphany**	*W*	Isaiah 49.1–7 Psalm 40.1–12 1 Corinthians 1.1–9 John 1.29–42	Psalm 145.1–12 Jeremiah 1.4–10 Mark 1.14–20	Psalm 96 Ezekiel 2.1—3.4 Galatians 1.11–end *HC John 1.43–end*	*DP* 96
			Holy Communion	Office	2nd Office or Alt HC	Psalmody
Monday	**14 January** DEL week 2	*W*	1 Samuel 15.16–23 Psalm 50.8–10, 16–17, 24 Mark 2.18–22	Genesis 7.1–23 Luke 5.1–11	1 Kings 7.13–26, 48–end Romans 5.1–11 *HC Ps 68.23–28; Mark 6.6b–13*	*MP* 93, 99, 150 *EP* 47, 48 *DP* 110
Tuesday	**15 January**	*W*	1 Samuel 16.1–13 Psalm 89.19–27 Mark 2.23–end	Genesis 8.6–end Luke 5.12–26	1 Kings 8.1–21 Romans 5.12–end *HC Ps 132.7–15; Mark 6.14–29*	*MP* 97, 146 *EP* 145 *DP* 111
Wednesday	**16 January**	*W*	1 Samuel 17.32–33, 37, 40–51 Psalm 144.1–2, 9–10 Mark 3.1–6	Genesis 9 Luke 5.27–end	1 Kings 8.22–30 Romans 6.1–14 *HC Ps 89.1–7; Mark 6.30–44*	*MP* 66, 147.13–end *EP* 81 *DP* 144
Thursday	**17 January** Antony of Egypt, hermit, abbot (see p.67) *Charles Gore, bishop*	*W*	1 Samuel 18.6–9; 19.1–7 Psalm 56.1–2, 8–end Mark 3.7–12	Genesis 11.1–9 Luke 6.1–11	1 Kings 8.54–end Romans 6.15–end *HC Ps 89.14–18; Mark 6.45–52*	*MP* 57, 148 *EP* 72, 98 *DP* 40
Friday	**18 January** *Week of Prayer for Christian Unity: 18–25 January*	*W*	1 Samuel 24.3–22*a* Psalm 57.1–2, 8–end Mark 3.13–19	Genesis 11.27—13.1 Luke 6.12–26	1 Kings 9.1–9 Romans 7.1–12 *HC Ps 89.30–35; Mark 6.53–end*	*MP* 24, 147.1–12 *EP* 36, 46 *DP* 46
Saturday	**19 January** Wulfstan, bishop (see p.67)	*W*	2 Samuel 1.1–4, 11–12, 17–19, 23–end Psalm 80.1–6 Mark 3.20–21	Genesis 13.2–end Luke 6.27–38	1 Kings 10.1–13 Romans 7.13–end *HC Ps 48.9–end; Mark 7.1–23*	*MP* 21, 149 *EP* 8, 20 *DP* 21

		Principal Service	3rd Service	2nd Service	Psalmody
Sunday	**20 January** *W* **3rd Sunday of Epiphany**	Isaiah 9.1–4 Psalm 27.1, 4–12 [*or* 27.1–11] 1 Corinthians 1.10–18 Matthew 4.12–23	Psalm 113 Amos 3.1–8 1 John 1.1–4	Psalm 33 [*or* 33.1–12] Ecclesiastes 3.1–11 1 Peter 1.3–12 *HC Luke 4.14–21*	*DP* 128
		Holy Communion	**Office**	**2nd Office or Alt HC**	**Psalmody**
Monday	**21 January** *Wr* Agnes, martyr (*see* p.65) DEL week 3	2 Samuel 5.1–7, 10 Psalm 89.19–27 Mark 3.22–30	Genesis 14.[1–7]8–24 Luke 6.39–end	1 Kings 15.9–15 Romans 8.1–17 *HC Ps 37.27–32; Mark 7.24–30*	*MP* 93, 99, 150 *EP* 47, 48 *DP* 93
Tuesday	**22 January** *W* *Vincent of Saragossa, deacon, martyr*	2 Samuel 6.12–15, 17–19 Psalm 24.7–end Mark 3.31–end	Genesis 15 Luke 7.1–17	1 Kings 17 Romans 8.18–27 *HC Ps 25.3–6; Mark 7.31–end*	*MP* 97, 146 *EP* 145 *DP* 24
Wednesday	**23 January** *W*	2 Samuel 7.4–17 Psalm 89.19–27 Mark 4.1–20	Genesis 16.1–14 Luke 7.18–35	1 Kings 18.20–39 Romans 8.28–end *HC Ps 57.1–6; Mark 8.1–10*	*MP* 66, 147.13–end *EP* 81 *DP* 66
Thursday	**24 January** *W* Francis de Sales, bishop, teacher of the faith (*see* p.66)	2 Samuel 7.18–19, 24–end Psalm 132.1–5, 11–15 Mark 4.21–25	Genesis 16.15—17.14 Luke 7.36–end	1 Kings 19.9*b*–18 Romans 10.1–17 *HC Ps 57.7–end; Mark 8.11–21*	*MP* 57, 148 *EP* 72, 98 *DP* 145
			or: 1st EP of Conversion of Paul: Psalm 149; Isaiah 49.1–13; Acts 22.3–16		
		Principal Service	**3rd Service**	**2nd Service**	**Psalmody**
Friday	**25 January** *W* Conversion of Paul	Jeremiah 1.4–10 *or* Acts 9.1–22 Psalm 67 Acts 9.1–22 *or* Galatians 1.11–16*a* Matthew 19.27–end	Ezekiel 3.22–end Philippians 3.1–14	Ecclesiasticus 39.1–10 *or* Isaiah 56.1–8 Colossians 1.24—2.7	*MP* 66, 147.13–end *EP* 119.41–56 *DP* 119.41–56
		Holy Communion	**Office**	**2nd Office or Alt HC**	**Psalmody**
Saturday	**26 January** *W* Timothy and Titus, companions of Paul	2 Samuel 12.1–7, 10–17 Psalm 51.11–16 Mark 4.35–end	Genesis 18 Luke 8.16–25	2 Kings 5.1–16 Romans 11.13–25, 33–end *HC Ps 34.5–9; Mark 8.27–33*	*MP* 21, 149 *EP* 8, 20 *DP* 51
		Lesser festival eucharistic lectionary: Isaiah 61.1–3*a*; Ps 100; 2 Timothy 2.1–5; Luke 10.1–9			

		Principal Service	3rd Service	2nd Service	Psalmody	
Sunday	**27 January** *W* **4th Sunday of Epiphany**	1 Kings 17.8–16 Psalm 36.5–10 1 Corinthians 1.18–end John 2.1–11	Psalm 71.1–6, 15–17 Haggai 2.1–9 1 Corinthians 3.10–17	Psalm 34 [*or* 34.1–10] Genesis 28.10–end Philemon 1–16 *HC Mark 1.21–28*	*DP* 5	
		Holy Communion	**Office**	**2nd Office or Alt HC**	**Psalmody**	**Alt Pss**
Monday	**28 January** *W* Thomas Aquinas, priest, teacher of the faith (*see* p.66); DEL week 4	2 Samuel 15.13–14, 30; 16.5–13 Psalm 3 Mark 5.1–20	Genesis 19.1–29 Luke 8.26–39	2 Kings 12.1–16 Romans 13 *HC Ps 13; Mark 8.34—9.1*	*MP* 93, 99, 150 *EP* 47, 48 *DP* 75	75, 76 77 81
Tuesday	**29 January** *W*	2 Samuel 18.9–10, 14, 24–25, 30—19.3 Psalm 86.1–6 Mark 5.21–end	Genesis 21.1–21 Luke 8.40–end	2 Kings 18.1–16 Romans 14.1–18 *HC Ps 115.12–end; Mark 9.2–8*	*MP* 97, 146 *EP* 145 *DP* 53	78.1–20 78.21–55 82
Wednesday	**30 January** *Wr* Charles, king and martyr (*see* p.65)	2 Samuel 24.2, 9–17 Psalm 32.1–8 Mark 6.1–6*a*	Genesis 22.1–18 Luke 9.1–17	2 Kings 19.14–19 Romans 14.19—15.6 *HC Ps 84.8–12; Mark 9.9–13*	*MP* 66, 147.13–end *EP* 81 *DP* 77	78.56–end 79 83
Thursday	**31 January** *W* *John Bosco, priest*	1 Kings 2.1–4, 10–12 *Canticle:* 1 Chronicles 29.10–12 *or* Psalm 145.1–5 Mark 6.7–13	Genesis 23 Luke 9.18–27	2 Kings 20.12–end Romans 15.7–22 *HC Ps 26.8–end; Mark 9.14–29*	*MP* 57, 148 *EP* 72, 98 *DP* 16	80 81 84
Friday	**1 February** *W* *Brigid, abbess*	Ecclesiasticus 47.2–11 Psalm 18.31–36, 50–end Mark 6.14–29	Genesis 24.1–27 Luke 9.28–36	2 Kings 22.1–13 Romans 15.23–end *HC Ps 44.21–end; Mark 9.30–32*	*MP* 24, 147.1–12 *EP* 36, 46 *DP* 54	82, 83 84 85, 86
			1st EP of Presentation: Psalm 118; 1 Samuel 1.19*b*–end; Hebrews 4.11–end			
		Principal Service	**3rd Service**	**2nd Service**	**Psalmody**	
Saturday	**2 February** *Gold or W* **Presentation of Christ in the Temple**	Malachi 3.1–5 Psalm 24.[1–6] 7–end Hebrews 2.14–end Luke 2.22–40	Exodus 13.1–16 Romans 12.1–5	Haggai 2.1–9 John 2.18–22	*MP* 48, 146 *EP* 122, 132 *DP* 122	
		Holy Communion	**Office**	**2nd Office or Alt HC**	**Psalmody**	**Alt Pss**
Saturday	**2 February** *W* *Or, when Presentation of Christ is celebrated on Sunday 3 February*	1 Kings 3.4–13 Psalm 119.9–16 Mark 6.30–34	Genesis 24.28–67 Luke 9.37–50	2 Kings 23.1–25 Romans 16.1–16 *HC Ps 37.7–11; Mark 9.33–37*	*MP* 21, 149 *EP* 118 *DP* 77	85, 86 87, 88 87, 88
			1st EP of Presentation: 1 Samuel 1.19*b*–end; Hebrews 4.11–end			

		Principal Service	3rd Service	2nd Service	Psalmody
Sunday	**3 February** *G* **2nd Sunday before Lent** Ordinary Time starts today	Genesis 1.1—2.3 Psalm 136 [*or* 1–9, 23–26] Romans 8.18–25 Matthew 6.25–34	Psalms 100, 150 Job 38.1–21 Colossians 1.15–20	Psalm 148 Proverbs 8.1, 22–31 Revelation 4 *HC Luke 12.16–31*	*DP* 1
	Or, if Presentation of Christ is being celebrated:				
Sunday	**3 February** *Gold or W* **Presentation of Christ in the Temple**	Malachi 3.1–5 Psalm 24.[1–6] 7–end Hebrews 2.14–end Luke 2.22–40	Exodus 13.1–16 Romans 12.1–5	Haggai 2.1–9 John 2.18–22	*MP* 48, 146 *EP* 122, 132 *DP* 122
		Holy Communion	**Office**	**2nd Office or Alt HC**	**Psalmody**
Monday	**4 February** *G* *Gilbert of Sempringham, abbot* DEL week 5	1 Kings 8.1–7, 9–13 Psalm 132.1–9 Mark 6.53–end	Genesis 25.19–end Luke 9.51–end	2 Kings 25 Romans 16.17–end *HC Ps 74.17–end; Mark 9.38–41*	*MP* 89.1–18 *EP* 89.19–37 *DP* 119.1–8
Tuesday	**5 February** *G*	1 Kings 8.22–23, 27–30 Psalm 84.1–10 Mark 7.1–13	Genesis 26.1–33 Luke 10.1–16	Nahum 1.1–8, 15 3 John *HC Ps 66.1–3; Mark 9.42–end*	*MP* 89.38–end *EP* 90 [91] *DP* 2
Wednesday	**6 February** *G* *Martyrs of Japan, 1597*	1 Kings 10.1–10 Psalm 37.3–6, 30–32 Mark 7.14–23	Genesis 27.1–29 Luke 10.17–24	Wisdom 6.1–11 *or* Deuteronomy 6.1–13 Titus 1.1–9 *HC Ps 2.7–11a; Mark 10.1–12*	*MP* 92, 93 *EP* 94 [96] *DP* 3
Thursday	**7 February** *G*	1 Kings 11.4–13 Psalm 106.3, 36–42 Mark 7.24–30	Genesis 27.30–45 Luke 10.25–37	Jonah 1 Titus 2.1–8, 11–14 *HC Ps 107.23–29; Mark 10.13–16*	*MP* [95] 97 *EP* 98, 99 *DP* 4
Friday	**8 February** *G*	1 Kings 11.29–32; 12.19 Psalm 81.8–14 Mark 7.31–end	Genesis 27.46—end of 28 Luke 10.38–end	Jonah 2 Titus 3.1–11 *HC Ps 130; Mark 10.17–22*	*MP* [100] 101 *EP* 102 *DP* 5
Saturday	**9 February** *G*	1 Kings 12.26–32; 13.33–end Psalm 106.6–7, 20–23 Mark 8.1–10	Genesis 29.1–30 Luke 11.1–13	Jonah 3, 4 Philemon *HC Ps 22.27–end; Mark 10.23–31*	*MP* [103] *or* 105.1–22 *EP* [104] *or* 105.23–end *DP* 6

		Principal Service	3rd Service	2nd Service	Psalmody
Sunday	**10 February** *G* **Sunday next before Lent**	Exodus 24.12–end Psalm 2 *or* 99 2 Peter 1.16–end Matthew 17.1–9	Psalm 72 Exodus 34.29–end 2 Corinthians 4.3–6	Psalm 84 Ecclesiasticus 48.1–10 *or* 2 Kings 2.1–12 Matthew 17.9–23 [*or* 1–23]	*DP* 24
		Holy Communion	**Office**	**2nd Office or Alt HC**	**Psalmody**
Monday	**11 February** *G* DEL week 6	James 1.1–11 Psalm 119.65–72 Mark 8.11–13	Proverbs 27.1–12 Jude 1–16	Job 5.8–end Luke 10.38–end *HC Ps 69.14–20*	*MP* 18.1–25 *EP* 18.26–end *DP* 119.33–40
Tuesday	**12 February** *G*	James 1.12–18 Psalm 94.12–18 Mark 8.14–21	Proverbs 30.1–4, 24–end Jude vv 17–end	Deuteronomy 8.11–end Luke 11.14–26 *HC Ps 105.7–11*	*MP* 20 *EP* 21 *DP* 25
		Principal Service	**3rd Service**	**2nd Service**	**Psalmody**
Wednesday	**13 February** *P(La)* Ash Wednesday	Joel 2.1–2, 12–17 *or* Isaiah 58.1–12 Psalm 51.1–18 2 Corinthians 5.20*b*—6.10 Matthew 6.1–6, 16–21 *or* John 8.1–11	Daniel 9.3–6, 17–19 1 Timothy 6.6–19	Isaiah 1.10–18 Luke 15.11–end	*MP* 38 *EP* 102 [*or* 102.1–18] *DP* 51
		Holy Communion	**Office**	**2nd Office or Alt HC**	**Psalmody**
Thursday	**14 February** *P(La)w* Cyril and Methodius, missionaries (see p.67) *Valentine, martyr*	Deuteronomy 30.15–end Psalm 1 Luke 9.22–25	Habakkuk 3.1–18 Luke 11.1–13	Ecclesiasticus 2.1–11 *or* Amos 5.6–12 Luke 11.27–36 *HC Ps 119.105–112*	*MP* 25 *EP* 27 *DP* 1
Friday	**15 February** *P(La)* *Sigfrid, bishop; Thomas Bray, priest*	Isaiah 58.1–9*a* Psalm 51.1–4, 16–17 Matthew 9.14–15	Ezekiel 18.1–4, 25–end Mark 2.13–20	Exodus 34.1–9, 27–29 Luke 11.37—12.1 *HC Ps 148.11–end*	*MP* 39 *EP* 69 *DP* 39
Saturday	**16 February** *P(La)*	Isaiah 58.9*b*–end Psalm 86.1–7 Luke 5.27–32	Ezekiel 39.21–end Mark 14.32–42	Joshua 23.1–8 Luke 12.2–12 *HC Ps 54*	*MP* 13, 124 *EP* 31 *DP* 86

		Principal Service	3rd Service	2nd Service	Psalmody
Sunday	**17 February** *P(La)* **1st Sunday of Lent**	Genesis 2.15–17; 3.1–7 Psalm 32 Romans 5.12–19 Matthew 4.1–11	Psalm 119.1–16 Jeremiah 18.1–11 Luke 18.9–14	Psalm 50.1–15 Deuteronomy 6.4–9, 16–end Luke 15.1–10	*DP* 32
		Holy Communion	Office	2nd Office or Alt HC	Psalmody
Monday	**18 February** *P(La)*	Leviticus 19.1–2, 11–18 Psalm 19.7–end Matthew 25.31–end	Genesis 37.1–11 1 Corinthians 1.1–19	Hosea 8.11–end; 10.1–2 Luke 12.13–21 *HC Ps 81.11–16*	*MP* 26, 32 *EP* 102 *DP* 26
Tuesday	**19 February** *P(La)*	Isaiah 55.10, 11 Psalm 34.4–6, 21–22 Matthew 6.7–15	Genesis 37.12–24 1 Corinthians 1.20–end	Deuteronomy 26.1–11 Luke 12.22–48 *HC Ps 106.1–5*	*MP* 56 *EP* 38 *DP* 34
Wednesday	**20 February** *P(La)* Ember Day (*see* p.6)	Jonah 3.1–10 Psalm 51.1–4, 16–17 Luke 11.29–32	Genesis 37.25–end 1 Corinthians 2.1–13	Leviticus 19.9–18 Luke 12.49–end *HC Ps 15*	*MP* 3, 6 *EP* 90 *DP* 3
Thursday	**21 February** *P(La)*	Esther 14.1–5, 12–14 *or* Isaiah 55.6–9 Psalm 138 Matthew 7.7–12	Genesis 39 1 Corinthians 2.14—3.15	Prayer of Manasseh *or* Jeremiah 8.4–12 Luke 13.1–9 *HC Ps 39.8–end*	*MP* 25 *EP* 27 *DP* 25
Friday	**22 February** *P(La)* Ember Day	Ezekiel 18.21–28 Psalm 130 Matthew 5.20–26	Genesis 40 1 Corinthians 3.16–end	Isaiah 29.17–end Luke 13.10–17 *HC Ps 25.7–11*	*MP* 39 *EP* 69 *DP* 130
Saturday	**23 February** *P(La)r* Polycarp, bishop, martyr (*see* p.65) Ember Day	Deuteronomy 26.16–end Psalm 119.1–8 Matthew 5.43–end	Genesis 41.1–24 1 Corinthians 4.1–7	Isaiah 49.8–16*a* Luke 13.18–end *HC Ps 97.6–end*	*MP* 13, 124 *EP* 31 *DP* 31

		Principal Service	3rd Service	2nd Service	Psalmody
Sunday	**24 February** *P(La)* **2nd Sunday of Lent**	Genesis 12.1–4*a* Psalm 121 Romans 4.1–5, 13–17 John 3.1–17	Psalm 74 Jeremiah 22.1–9 Matthew 8.1–13	Psalm 135 [*or* 135.1–14] Numbers 21.4–9 Luke 14.27–33	*DP* 121

		Holy Communion	Office	2nd Office or Alt HC	Psalmody
Monday	**25 February** *P(La)*	Daniel 9.4–10 Psalm 79.8–9, 12, 14 Luke 6.36–38	Genesis 41.25–end 1 Corinthians 4.8–21	2 Kings 20.1–11 Luke 14.1–14 *HC Ps 13*	*MP* 26, 32 *EP* 102 *DP* 12
Tuesday	**26 February** *P(La)*	Isaiah 1.10, 16–20 Psalm 50.8, 16–end Matthew 23.1–12	Genesis 42.1–17 1 Corinthians 5.1–8	Isaiah 57.14–end Luke 14.15–24 *HC Ps 32.9–end*	*MP* 56 *EP* 38 *DP* 116
Wednesday	**27 February** *P(La)w* George Herbert, priest, poet (see p.66)	Jeremiah 18.18–20 Psalm 31.4–5, 14–18 Matthew 20.17–28	Genesis 42.18–28 1 Corinthians 5.9—6.8	Numbers 27.15–end Luke 14.25–end *HC Ps 77.16–20*	*MP* 3, 6 *EP* 90 *DP* 108
Thursday	**28 February** *P(La)*	Jeremiah 17.5–10 Psalm 1 Luke 16.19–end	Genesis 42.29–end 1 Corinthians 6.9–20	Joel 2.12–17 Luke 15.1–10 *HC Ps 88.9–15*	*MP* 25 *EP* 27 *DP* 92
Friday	**1 March** *P(La)w* David, bishop, patron of Wales (see p.66)	Genesis 37.3–4, 12–13, 17–28 Psalm 105.16–22 Matthew 21.33–43, 45–46	Genesis 43.1–15 1 Corinthians 7.1–9	Song of the Three vv 1–14 *or* Hosea 6.1–6 Luke 15.11–end *HC Ps 104.26–32*	*MP* 39 *EP* 69 *DP* 69
Saturday	**2 March** *P(La)w* Chad, bishop, missionary (see p.67)	Micah 7.14–15, 18–20 Psalm 103.1–4, 9–12 Luke 15.1–3, 11–end	Genesis 43.16–end 1 Corinthians 7.10–24	Micah 6.1–8 Luke 16.1–13 *HC Ps 19.7–10*	*MP* 13, 124 *EP* 31 *DP* 13

		Principal Service	3rd Service	2nd Service	Psalmody
Sunday	**3 March** *P(La)* **3rd Sunday of Lent**	Exodus 17.1–7 Psalm 95 Romans 5.1–11 John 4.5–42	Psalm 46 Amos 7.10–end 2 Corinthians 1.1–11	Psalm 40 Joshua 1.1–9 Ephesians 6.10–20 *HC John 2.13–22*	*DP* 95

The following readings may replace those provided for Holy Communion on any day during the 3rd week of Lent: Exodus 17.1–7; Psalm 95.1–2, 6–end; John 4.5–42

		Holy Communion	Office	2nd Office or Alt HC	Psalmody
Monday	**4 March** *P(La)*	2 Kings 5.1–15 Psalms 42.1–2; 43.1–4 Luke 4.24–30	Genesis 44.1–17 1 Corinthians 7.25–31	Deuteronomy 32.1–14 Luke 16.14–18 *HC Ps 18.1–7*	*MP* 26, 32 *EP* 102 *DP* 42
Tuesday	**5 March** *P(La)*	Song of the Three, vv 2, 11–20 *or* Daniel 2.20–23 Psalm 25.3–10 Matthew 18.21–end	Genesis 44.18–end 1 Corinthians 7.32–end	Daniel 12.1–9 Luke 16.19–end *HC Ps 16.7–end*	*MP* 56 *EP* 38 *DP* 43
Wednesday	**6 March** *P(La)*	Deuteronomy 4.1, 5–9 Psalm 147.13–end Matthew 5.17–19	Genesis 45 1 Corinthians 8	2 Kings 6.8–17 Luke 17.1–10 *HC Ps 28.7–end*	*MP* 3, 6 *EP* 90 *DP* 6
Thursday	**7 March** *P(La)r* Perpetua, Felicity and companions, martyrs (see p.65)	Jeremiah 7.23–28 Psalm 95.1–2, 6–end Luke 11.14–23	Genesis 46.1–7, 28–end 1 Corinthians 9.1–15	Song of the Three, vv 29–34 *or* 2 Kings 5.9–14 Luke 17.11–19 *HC Ps 104.33–end*	*MP* 25 *EP* 27 *DP* 27
Friday	**8 March** *P(La)w* Edward King, bishop (see p.66) *Felix, bishop;* *Geoffrey Studdert Kennedy, priest, poet*	Hosea 14.2–10 Psalm 81.6–10, 13, 16 Mark 12.28–34	Genesis 47 1 Corinthians 9.16–end	Isaiah 33.17–22 Luke 17.20–end *HC Ps 125*	*MP* 39 *EP* 69 *DP* 81
Saturday	**9 March** *P(La)*	Hosea 5.15—6.6 Psalm 51.1–2, 16–end Luke 18.9–14	Genesis 48 1 Corinthians 10.1–13	Ezekiel 12.21–end Luke 18.1–8 *HC Ps 71.1–6*	*MP* 13, 124 *EP* 31 *DP* 51

			Principal Service	3rd Service	2nd Service	Psalmody
Sunday	**10 March** **4th Sunday of Lent** *Mothering Sunday*	*P(La)*	1 Samuel 16.1–13 Psalm 23 Ephesians 5.8–14 John 9	Psalm 19 Isaiah 43.1–7 Ephesians 2.8–14	Psalm 31.1–16 *or* 31.1–8 Micah 7 *or* Prayer of Manasseh James 5 *HC John 3.14–21*	*DP* 23

For Mothering Sunday:
Exodus 2.1–10 *or* 1 Samuel 1.20–end; Psalm 34.11–20 *or* Psalm 127; 2 Corinthians 1.3–7 *or* Colossians 3.12–17; Luke 2.33–35 *or* John 19.25*b*–27.
If the Principal Service readings have been displaced by Mothering Sunday provisions, they may be used at the Second Service.

The following readings may replace those provided for Holy Communion on any day during the 4th week of Lent: Micah 7.7–9; Psalm 27.1, 9–10, 16–17; John 9

			Holy Communion	Office	2nd Office or Alt HC	Psalmody
Monday	**11 March**	*P(La)*	Isaiah 65.17–21 Psalm 30.1–5, 8, 11–12 John 4.43–end	Genesis 49.1–28 1 Corinthians 10.14—11.1	Amos 5.6–15 Luke 18.9–14 *HC Ps 119.137–142*	*MP* 26, 32 *EP* 102 *DP* 30
Tuesday	**12 March**	*P(La)*	Ezekiel 47.1–9, 12 Psalm 46.1–8 John 5.1–3, 5–16	Genesis 49.29—50.14 1 Corinthians 11.2–16	Exodus 20.1–17 Luke 18.15–30 *HC Ps 119.1–6*	*MP* 56 *EP* 38 *DP* 47
Wednesday	**13 March**	*P(La)*	Isaiah 49.8–15 Psalm 145.8–17 John 5.17–30	Genesis 50.15–end 1 Corinthians 11.17–end	Isaiah 53.7–end Luke 18.31–end *HC Ps 130*	*MP* 3, 6 *EP* 90 *DP* 145
Thursday	**14 March**	*P(La)*	Exodus 32.7–14 Psalm 106.19–23 John 5.31–47	Exodus 1.6–end 1 Corinthians 12.1–11	Ecclesiasticus 15.15–end *or* Joshua 24.14–28 Luke 19.1–10 *HC Ps 119.113–120*	*MP* 25 *EP* 27 *DP* 106.1–24
Friday	**15 March**	*P(La)*	Wisdom 2.1, 12–22 *or* Jeremiah 26.8–11 Psalm 34.15–end John 7.1–2, 10, 25–30	Exodus 2 1 Corinthians 12.12–26	Proverbs 4.1–13 Luke 19.11–27 *HC Ps 119.17–24*	*MP* 39 *EP* 69 *DP* 106.25–50
Saturday	**16 March**	*P(La)*	Jeremiah 11.18–20 Psalm 7.1–2, 8–10 John 7.40–52	Exodus 3 1 Corinthians 12.27—13.3	Zechariah 9.9–12 Luke 19.28–38 *HC Ps 72.1–8*	*MP* 13, 124 *EP* 13, 130 *DP* 7

		Principal Service	3rd Service	2nd Service	Psalmody
Sunday	**17 March** *P(La)* **5th Sunday of Lent** *Passiontide begins*	Ezekiel 37.1–14 Psalm 130 Romans 8.6–11 John 11.1–45	Psalm 86 Jeremiah 31.27–37 John 12.20–33	Psalm 30 Lamentations 3.19–33 Matthew 20.17–end	*DP* 126

The following readings may replace those provided for Holy Communion on any day during the 5th week of Lent: 2 Kings 4.18–21, 32–37; Psalm 17.1–8, 16; John 11.1–45

		Holy Communion	Office	2nd Office or Alt HC	Psalmody
Monday	**18 March** *P(La)* *Cyril, bishop, teacher of the faith*	Susanna 1–9, 15–17, 19–30, 33–62 [*or* 41–62] *or* Joshua 2.1–14 Psalm 23 John 8.1–11	Exodus 4 1 Corinthians 13	Jeremiah 7.1–11 Luke 19.39–end *HC Ps 14*	*MP* 73 *EP* 26, 27 *DP* 73

or: 1st EP of Joseph of Nazareth:
Psalm 132; Hosea 11.1–9; Luke 2.41–end

		Principal Service	3rd Service	2nd Service	Psalmody
Tuesday	**19 March** *W* Joseph of Nazareth	2 Samuel 7.4–16 Psalm 89.26–36 Romans 4.13–18 Matthew 1.18–end	Isaiah 11.1–10 Matthew 13.54–end	Genesis 50.22–end Matthew 2.13–end	*MP* 25, 147.1–12 *EP* 1, 112 *DP* 1

		Holy Communion	Office	2nd Office or Alt HC	Psalmody
Wednesday	**20 March** *P(La)w* Cuthbert, bishop, missionary (see p.67)	Daniel 3.14–20, 24–25, 28 Song of the Three vv 29–34 *or* Psalm 104.1–7 John 8.31–42	Exodus 7.8–24 1 Corinthians 14.20–end	Genesis 22.1–18 Luke 20.9–19 *HC Ps 28.7–end*	*MP* 55 *EP* 56, 62 *DP* 55
Thursday	**21 March** *P(La)r* Thomas Cranmer, archbishop, martyr	Genesis 17.3–9 Psalm 105.4–9 John 8.51–end	Exodus 7.25—8.19 1 Corinthians 16.1–9	Isaiah 45.1–7 Luke 20.20–26 *HC Ps 99.1–5*	*MP* 40, 54 *EP* 42, 43 *DP* 105
Friday	**22 March** *P(La)*	Jeremiah 20.10–13 Psalm 18.1–6 John 10.31–end	Exodus 9.13–end 1 Corinthians 16.10–end	2 Kings 4.18–37 Luke 20.27–40 *HC Ps 34.15–18*	*MP* 69 *EP* 31 *DP* 18.1–31
Saturday	**23 March** *P(La)*	Ezekiel 37.21–28 *Canticle:* Jeremiah 31.10–13 *or* Psalm 121 John 11.45–end	Exodus 10.21—11.8 John 2.19–end	2 Samuel 7.4–16 Luke 20.41—21.4 *HC Ps 132.14–end*	*MP* 23, 88 *EP* 13, 130 *DP* 18.32–end

Day	Date		Principal Service		3rd Service	2nd Service	Psalmody
Sunday	**24 March** **Palm Sunday**	*R*	*Liturgy of the Palms:* Matthew 21.1–11 Psalm 118.1–2, 19–29 [*or* 118.19–24]	*Liturgy of the Passion:* Isaiah 50.4–9*a* Psalm 31.9–16 [*or* 31.9–18] Philippians 2.5–11 Matthew 26.14—end of 27 *or* Matthew 27.11–54	Psalms 61, 62 Zechariah 9.9–12 Luke 16.19–end	Psalm 80 Isaiah 5.1–7 Matthew 21.33–end	*DP* 51

Day	Date		Principal Service	3rd Service	2nd Service	Psalmody
Monday	**25 March** Monday of Holy Week	*R*	Isaiah 42.1–9 Psalm 36.5–11 Hebrews 9.11–15 John 12.1–11	Psalm 25 Lamentations 2.8–19 Colossians 1.18–23	Psalm 41 Lamentations 1.1–12*a* Luke 22.1–23	*DP* 41
	The Annunciation of Our Lord to the Blessed Virgin Mary *is transferred from 25 March to 8 April in 2002.*					
Tuesday	**26 March** Tuesday of Holy Week	*R*	Isaiah 49.1–7 Psalm 71.1–14 [*or* 71.1–8] 1 Corinthians 1.18–31 John 12.20–36	Psalm 55.13–24 Lamentations 3.40–51 Galatians 6.11–end	Psalm 27 Lamentations 3.1–18 Luke 22.24–53 [*or* 39–53]	*DP* 71
Wednesday	**27 March** Wednesday of Holy Week	*R*	Isaiah 50.4–9*a* Psalm 70 Hebrews 12.1–3 John 13.21–32	Psalm 88 Isaiah 63.1–9 Revelation 14.18—15.4	Psalm 102 [*or* 102.1–18] Wisdom 1.16—2.1, 2.12–22 *or* Jeremiah 11.18–20 Luke 22.54–end	*DP* 88
Thursday	**28 March** **Maundy Thursday**	*W*	Exodus 12.1–4 [5–10], 11–14 Psalm 116.1, 10–17 [*or* 116.9–17] 1 Corinthians 11.23–26 John 13.1–17, 31*b*–35	Exodus 11 Ephesians 2.11–18	Leviticus 16.2–24 Luke 23.1–25	*MP* 42, 43 *EP* 39 *DP* 116
Friday	**29 March** **Good Friday** *Red for the Liturgy*	*Hangings removed*	Isaiah 52.13—end of 53 Psalm 22 [*or* 22.1–11 *or* 21] Hebrews 10.16–25 *or* Hebrews 4.14–16; 5.7–9 John 18.1—end of 19	Lamentations 5.15–end *or* Hebrews 10.1–10	Genesis 22.1–18 John 19.38–end *or* Colossians 1.18–23	*MP* 69 *EP* 130, 143 *DP* 22

A part of John 18 and 19 may be read, especially in the evening, if not used at the Principal Service.

Day	Date	Colour	Principal Service	3rd Service	2nd Service	Psalmody
Saturday	**30 March** Easter Eve *These readings are for use at services other than the Easter Vigil.*	*Hangings removed*	Job 14.1–14 *or* Lamentations 3.1–9, 19–24 Psalm 31.1–4, 15–16 [*or* 31.1–5] 1 Peter 4.1–8 Matthew 27.57–end *or* John 19.38–end	Psalm 116 Job 19.21–27 1 John 5.5–12	Psalm 142 Hosea 6.1–6 John 2.18–22	*DP* 142
Saturday *or* **Sunday**	**30 March evening** **31 March morning** *Easter Vigil*	*Gold or W*	*A minimum of three Old Testament readings should be chosen. The Exodus reading and canticle should always be used.* Genesis 1.1—2.4*a* Genesis 7.1–5, 11–18; 8.6–18; 9.8–13 Genesis 22.1–18 **Exodus 14.10–end; 15.20–21** Isaiah 55.1–11 Baruch 3.9–15, 32—4.4 *or* Proverbs 8.1–8, 19–21; 9.4*b*–6 Ezekiel 36.24–28 Ezekiel 37.1–14 Zephaniah 3.14–end **Romans 6.3–11** **Matthew 28.1–10**	 Psalm 136.1–9, 23–26 Psalm 46 Psalm 16 *Canticle*: **Exodus 15.1*b*–13, 17–18** *Canticle:* Isaiah 12.2–6 Psalm 19 Psalms 42, 43 Psalm 143 Psalm 98 **Psalm 114**		

Day	Date	Colour	Principal Service	3rd Service	2nd Service	Psalmody
Sunday	**31 March** Easter Day	*Gold or W*	Acts 10.34–43 *or* Jeremiah 31.1–6 Psalm 118.1–2, 14–24 [*or* 118.14–24] Colossians 3.1–4 *or* Acts 10.34–43 John 20.1–18 *or* Matthew 28.1–10	Exodus 14.10–18, 26—15.2 Revelation 15.2–4	Song of Solomon 3.2–5; 8.6–7 John 20.11–18 *if not used at the Principal Service,* *or* Revelation 1.12–18	*MP* 114, 117 *EP* 105, *or* 66.1–11 *DP* 118

Easter Week

		Holy Communion	Office	2nd Office	Psalmody
	During Easter week the Second Office lectionary may not be used as an alternative eucharistic lectionary.				
Monday	**1 April** *W* Monday in Easter Week	Acts 2.14, 22–32 Psalm 16.1–2, 6–end Matthew 28.8–15	Exodus 12.14–27 1 Corinthians 15.1–11	Jonah 2.1–9 Mark 16.1–8	*MP* 2, 110, 149 *EP* 3, 135 *DP* 135
Tuesday	**2 April** *W* Tuesday in Easter Week	Acts 2.36–41 Psalm 33.4–5, 18–end John 20.11–18	Exodus 12.28–39 1 Corinthians 15.12–28	Isaiah 30.18–21 Mark 16.9–end	*MP* 63, 146 *EP* 118 *DP* 146
Wednesday	**3 April** *W* Wednesday in Easter Week	Acts 3.1–10 Psalm 105.1–9 Luke 24.13–35	Exodus 12.40–end 1 Corinthians 15.30–41	Micah 7.7–15 Matthew 28.1–15	*MP* 57, 147.13–end *EP* 113, 117 *DP* 113
Thursday	**4 April** *W* Thursday in Easter Week	Acts 3.11–end Psalm 8 Luke 24.35–48	Exodus 13.1–16 1 Corinthians 15.41–50	Ezekiel 37.1–14 Matthew 28.16–end	*MP* 30, 148 *EP* 111, 116 *DP* 114
Friday	**5 April** *W* Friday in Easter Week	Acts 4.1–12 Psalm 118.1–4, 22–26 John 21.1–14	Exodus 13.17—14.4 1 Corinthians 15.51–end	Daniel 12.1–4, 13 Luke 24.1–12	*MP* 29, 147.1–12 *EP* 114, 115 *DP* 115
Saturday	**6 April** *W* Saturday in Easter Week	Acts 4.13–21 Psalm 118.1–4, 14–21 Mark 16.9–15	Exodus 14.5–22 2 Corinthians 4.16—5.10	Isaiah 25.1–9 Mark 12.18–27	*MP* 103, 150 *EP* 136 *DP* 103

		Principal Service	3rd Service	2nd Service	Psalmody
Sunday	**7 April** *W* **2nd Sunday of Easter**	[Exodus 14.10–end; 15.20–21] Acts 2.14*a*, 22–32 Psalm 16 1 Peter 1.3–9 John 20.19–end	Psalm 81.1–10 Exodus 12.1–17 1 Corinthians 5.6*b*–8	Psalm 30.1–5 Daniel 6.1–23 [*or* 6–23] Mark 15.46—16.8	*DP* 133
			Or: 1st EP of Annunciation of Our Lord Psalm 85; Wisdom 9.1–12 *or* Genesis 3.8–15; Galatians 4.1–5		
Monday	**8 April** *Gold or W* **Annunciation of our Lord to the BVM** *(transferred from 25 March)*	Isaiah 7.10–14 Psalm 40.5–11 Hebrews 10.4–10 Luke 1.26–38	1 Samuel 2.1–10 Romans 5.12–end	Isaiah 52.1–12 Hebrews 2.5–end	*MP* 111, 113 *EP* 131, 146 *DP* 131
		Holy Communion	**Office**	**2nd Office or Alt HC**	**Psalmody**
Tuesday	**9 April** *W* *Dietrich Bonhoeffer, pastor, martyr*	Acts 4.32–end Psalm 93 John 3.7–15	Exodus 15.1–21 Hebrews 2.1–10	Leviticus 23.1–14 1 Peter 1.25*b*—end of 2 *HC Ps 66.16–20; Matt 28.1–10*	*MP* 135, 146 *EP* 105.23–end *DP* 93
Wednesday	**10 April** *W* William Law, priest, spiritual writer (see p.66) *William of Ockham, friar, teacher of the faith*	Acts 5.17–26 Psalm 34.1–8 John 3.16–21	Exodus 15.22—16.10 Hebrews 2.11–end	Leviticus 25.1–17 1 Peter 3.8–end *HC Ps 102.16–21; Matt 28.11–end*	*MP* 139, 147.13–end *EP* 103 *DP* 34
Thursday	**11 April** *W* *George Selwyn, bishop*	Acts 5.27–33 Psalm 34.1, 15–end John 3.31–end	Exodus 16.10–22 Hebrews 3	Numbers 6.1–8 1 Peter 4.1–11 *HC Ps 56.10–end; Luke 24.1–12*	*MP* 33, 148 *EP* 136 *DP* 33
Friday	**12 April** *W*	Acts 5.34–end Psalm 27.1–5, 16–end John 6.1–15	Exodus 16.23–36 Hebrews 4.1–13	Numbers 22.21–35 1 Peter 4.12–end *HC Ps 81.11–end; Luke 24.13–35*	*MP* 30, 147.1–12 *EP* 107.33–end *DP* 147
Saturday	**13 April** *W*	Acts 6.1–7 Psalm 33.1–5, 18–19 John 6.16–21	Exodus 17 Hebrews 4.14—5.6	Numbers 28.16–end 1 Peter 5 *HC Ps 66.12–17; Luke 24.36–end*	*MP* 118, 149 *EP* 116 *DP* 149

			Principal Service	3rd Service	2nd Service	Psalmody
Sunday	**14 April** **3rd Sunday of Easter**	*W*	[Zephaniah 3.14–20] Acts 2.14*a*, 36–41 Psalm 116.1–3, 10–17 [*or* 116.1–7] 1 Peter 1.17–23 Luke 24.13–35	Psalm 23 Isaiah 40.1–11 1 Peter 5.1–11	Psalm 48 Haggai 1.13—2.9 1 Corinthians 3.10–17 *HC John 2.13–22*	*DP* 116, 117

			Holy Communion	Office	2nd Office or Alt HC	Psalmody
Monday	**15 April**	*W*	Acts 6.8–end Psalm 119.17–24 John 6.22–29	Exodus 18 Hebrews 5.7–end	Isaiah 51.1–6 2 Corinthians 1.1–12 *HC Ps 98.5–end; John 20.1–10*	*MP* 81, 150 *EP* 113, 115 *DP* 82
Tuesday	**16 April** *Isabella Gilmore, deaconess*	*W*	Acts 7.51—8.1 Psalm 31.1–5, 16 John 6.30–35	Exodus 19 Hebrews 6.1–12	Proverbs 15.23–end 2 Corinthians 1.13—2.4 *HC Ps 119.65–72; John 20.11–18*	*MP* 135, 146 *EP* 105.1–22 *DP* 74
Wednesday	**17 April**	*W*	Acts 8.1–8 Psalm 66.1–6 John 6.35–40	Exodus 20.1–21 Hebrews 6.13–end	Daniel 9.3–10 2 Corinthians 2.5–end *HC Ps 119.105–112; John 20.19–end*	*MP* 139, 147.13–end *EP* 103 *DP* 101
Thursday	**18 April**	*W*	Acts 8.26–end Psalm 66.7–8, 14–end John 6.44–51	Exodus 24 Hebrews 7.1–17	Exodus 34.29–end 2 Corinthians 3 *HC Ps 103.6–12; John 21.1–14*	*MP* 33, 148 *EP* 136 *DP* 136
Friday	**19 April** Alphege, archbishop, martyr (*see* p.65)	*Wr*	Acts 9.1–20 Psalm 117 John 6.52–59	Exodus 25.1–22 Hebrews 7.18–end	Job 10.2–9 2 Corinthians 4 *HC Ps 17.1–5; John 21.15–25*	*MP* 30, 147.1–12 *EP* 107.1–32 *DP* 107.1–32
Saturday	**20 April**	*W*	Acts 9.31–42 Psalm 116.10–15 John 6.60–69	Exodus 28.1–5 [6–29] 30–38 Hebrews 8	Wisdom 9.1–11 *or* 1 Kings 3.5–9 2 Corinthians 5.1–16 *HC Ps 119.145–152; Luke 1.1–25*	*MP* 118, 149 *EP* 116 *DP* 99

			Principal Service	**3rd Service**	**2nd Service**	**Psalmody**
Sunday	**21 April** **4th Sunday of Easter**	*W*	[Genesis 7] Acts 2.42–end Psalm 23 1 Peter 2.19–end John 10.1–10	Psalm 106.6–24 Nehemiah 9.6–15 1 Corinthians 10.1–13	Psalm 29 Ezra 3 Ephesians 2.11–end *HC Luke 19.37–end*	*DP* 148
			Holy Communion	**Office**	**2nd Office or Alt HC**	**Psalmody**
Monday	**22 April**	*W*	Acts 11.1–18 Psalms 42.1–2; 43.1–4 John 10.1–10 [*or* 11–18]	Exodus 32.1–20 Hebrews 9.1–14	Ezra 1.1–8, 11 2 Corinthians 5.17—6.2 *HC Ps 122.1–5; Luke 1.26–38*	*MP* 81, 150 *EP* 113, 115 *DP* 79
				or: 1st EP of George: Psalms 111, 116; Jeremiah 15.15–end; Hebrews 11.32—12.2		
			Principal Service	**3rd Service**	**2nd Service**	**Psalmody**
Tuesday	**23 April** George, martyr, patron of England	*R*	1 Maccabees 2.59–64 *or* Revelation 12.7–12 Psalm 126 2 Timothy 2.3–13 John 15.18–21	Joshua 1.1–9 Ephesians 6.10–20	Isaiah 43.1–7 John 15.1–8	*MP* 5, 146 *EP* 3, 11 *DP* 3
			Holy Communion	**Office**	**2nd Office or Alt HC**	**Psalmody**
Wednesday	**24 April** *Mellitus, bishop*	*W*	Acts 12.24–13.5 Psalm 67 John 12.44–end	Exodus 33 Hebrews 10.1–10	Nehemiah 1 2 Corinthians 8.1–15 *HC Ps 79.1–6; Luke 1.57–80*	*MP* 139, 147.13–end *EP* 103 *DP* 35
				or: 1st EP of Mark the Evangelist: Psalm 19; Isaiah 52.7–10; Mark 1.1–15		
			Principal Service	**3rd Service**	**2nd Service**	**Psalmody**
Thursday	**25 April** Mark the Evangelist	*R*	Proverbs 15.28–end *or* Acts 15.35–end Psalm 119.9–16 Ephesians 4.7–16 Mark 13.5–13	Isaiah 62.6–10 *or* Ecclesiasticus 51.13–end Acts 12.25—13.13	Ezekiel 1.4–14 2 Timothy 4.1–11	*MP* 37.23–41, 148 *EP* 45 *DP* 45
			Holy Communion	**Office**	**2nd Office or Alt HC**	**Psalmody**
Friday	**26 April**	*W*	Acts 13.26–33 Psalm 2 John 14.1–6	Exodus 34.18–end Hebrews 10.26–end	Nehemiah 2.11–end 2 Corinthians 9.6–end *HC Ps 75.1–5; Luke 2.21–40*	*MP* 30, 147.1–12 *EP* 107.33–43 *DP* 89.19–52
Saturday	**27 April** *Christina Rossetti, poet*	*W*	Acts 13.44–end Psalm 98.1–5 John 14.7–14	Exodus 40.18–end Hebrews 11.1–16	Nehemiah 4.7–end 2 Corinthians 10 *HC Ps 120; Luke 2.41–end*	*MP* 118, 149 *EP* 116 *DP* 98

Day	Date	Principal Service	3rd Service	2nd Service	Psalmody
Sunday	**28 April** W **5th Sunday of Easter**	[Genesis 8.1–19] Acts 7.55–end Psalm 31.1–5, 15–16 [*or* 31.1–5] 1 Peter 2.2–10 John 14.1–14	Psalm 30 Ezekiel 37.1–12 John 5.19–29	Psalm 147.1–12 Zechariah 4.1–10 Revelation 21.1–14 *HC Luke 2.25–32* [*33–38*]	*DP* 94

Day	Date	Holy Communion	Office	2nd Office or Alt HC	Psalmody
Monday	**29 April** W Catherine of Siena, teacher of the faith (see p.66)	Acts 14.5–18 Psalm 118.1–3, 14–15 John 14.21–26	Leviticus 8.1–13, 30–end Hebrews 11.17–31	Nehemiah 5.1–15 2 Corinthians 11.1–15 *HC Ps 125; Luke 3.1–6*	*MP* 81, 150 *EP* 113, 115 *DP* 63
Tuesday	**30 April** W *Pandita Mary Ramabai, translator*	Acts 14.19–end Psalm 145.10–end John 14.27–end	Leviticus 16.1–19 Hebrews 11.32—12.2	Nehemiah 7.73*b*—8.3; 8.8–12 2 Corinthians 11.16–end *HC Ps 100; Luke 3.7–22*	*MP* 135, 146 *EP* 105.1–22 *DP* 11
			or: 1st EP of Philip & James: Psalm 25; Isaiah 40.27–end; John 12.20–26		

Day	Date	Principal Service	3rd Service	2nd Service	Psalmody
Wednesday	**1 May** R Philip and James, apostles	Isaiah 30.15–21 Psalm 119.1–8 Ephesians 1.3–10 John 14.1–14	Proverbs 4.10–18 James 1.1–12	Job 23.1–12 John 1.43–end	*MP* 139, 146 *EP* 149 *DP* 139

Day	Date	Holy Communion	Office	2nd Office or Alt HC	Psalmody
Thursday	**2 May** W Athanasius, bishop, teacher of the faith (see p.66)	Acts 15.7–21 Psalm 96.1–3, 7–10 John 15.9–11	Leviticus 19.1–18 Hebrews 12.12–end	Ecclesiasticus 34.9–17 *or* Nehemiah 9.26–31 2 Corinthians 13 *HC Ps 119.121–128; Luke 4.14–30*	*MP* 33, 148 *EP* 136 *DP* 19
Friday	**3 May** W	Acts 15.22–31 Psalm 57.8–end John 15.12–17	Leviticus 19.26–end Hebrews 13.1–16	Exodus 3.1–17 1 Timothy 1.1–11 *HC Ps 99.1–5; Luke 4.31–end*	*MP* 30, 147.1–12 *EP* 107.1–32 *DP* 38
Saturday	**4 May** W English saints and martyrs of the Reformation era	Acts 16.1–10 Psalm 100 John 15.18–21	Leviticus 23.22–end Hebrews 13.17–end	Exodus 5.1–9; 5.22—6.1 1 Timothy 1.12–end *HC Ps 10.1–4; Luke 5.1–11*	*MP* 118, 149 *EP* 116 *DP* 100
		Lesser festival eucharistic lectionary: Isaiah 43.1–7 *or* Ecclesiasticus 2.10–17; Psalm 87; 2 Corinthians 4.5–12; John 12.20–26			

		Principal Service	3rd Service	2nd Service	Psalmody
Sunday	**5 May** *W* **6th Sunday of Easter**	[Genesis 8.20—9.17] Acts 17.22–31 Psalm 66.7–end 1 Peter 3.13–end John 14.15–21	Psalm 73.21–end Job 14.1–2, 7–15; 19.23–27*a* 1 Thessalonians 4.13–end	Psalms 87, 36.5–10 Zechariah 8.1–13 Revelation 21.22—22.5 *HC John 21.1–14*	*DP* 87
		Holy Communion	**Office**	**2nd Office or Alt HC**	**Psalmody**
Monday	**6 May** *W* Rogation Day (see p.69)	Acts 16.11–15 Psalm 149.1–5 John 15.26—16.4	Leviticus 25.1–17 1 John 1	Exodus 6.2–13 1 Timothy 2 *HC Ps 116.1–3; Luke 5.12–26*	*MP* 81, 150 *EP* 113, 115 *DP* 44
Tuesday	**7 May** *W* Rogation Day	Acts 16.22–34 Psalm 138 John 16.5–11	Leviticus 25.35–end 1 John 2.1–11	Exodus 7.8–end 1 Timothy 3.1–13 *HC Ps 105.23–27; Luke 5.27–end*	*MP* 135, 146 *EP* 105.23–end *DP* 14
Wednesday	**8 May** *W* Julian of Norwich, spiritual writer (see p.67) Rogation Day	Acts 17.15, 22—18.1 Psalm 148.1–2, 11–end John 16.12–15	Leviticus 26.1–20, 27–42 1 John 2.12–17	Exodus 8.1–5, 16–24 1 Timothy 3.14–end, 4.11–end *HC Ps 109.25–end; Luke 6.1–11*	*MP* 139, 147.13–end *EP* 15, 24 *DP* 15
				1st EP of Ascension Day: 2 Samuel 23.1–5; Colossians 2.20—3.4	
		Principal Service	**3rd Service**	**2nd Service**	**Psalmody**
Thursday	**9 May** *Gold or W* **Ascension Day**	Acts 1.1–11 *or* Daniel 7.9–14 Psalm 47 *or* 93 Ephesians 1.15–end *or* Acts 1.1–11 Luke 24.44–end	Isaiah 52.7–end Hebrews 7.[11–25] 26–end	Song of the Three, vv 29–37 *or* 2 Kings 2.1–15 Revelation 5 *HC Mark 16.14–end*	*MP* 110, 150 *EP* 8 *DP* 8
		Holy Communion	**Office**	**2nd Office or Alt HC**	**Psalmody**
	*From 10–18 May an alternative sequence of daily readings for use at the 2nd Office, in preparation for the Day of Pentecost, is marked with an asterisk *.*				
Friday	**10 May** *W*	Acts 18.9–18 Psalm 47.1–6 John 16.20–23	1 Samuel 2.1–10 1 John 2.18–end	Exodus 9.1–12 1 Timothy 5.17–22 *HC Ps 77.11–15; Luke 6.12–19* **Exod 35.30—36.1; Gal 5.13–end*	*MP* 139, 149 *EP* 84, 138 *DP* 47
Saturday	**11 May** *W*	Acts 18.23–end Psalm 47.1–2, 7–end John 16.23–28	Numbers 11.16–29 1 John 3.1–10	Exodus 9.22–end 1 Timothy 6 *HC Ps 144.5–8; Luke 6.20–26* **Ezek 18.1–4, 19–end; 1 Cor 2*	*MP* 92, 148 *EP* 93, 97, 98 *DP* 92

			Principal Service	3rd Service	2nd Service	Psalmody
Sunday	**12 May** **7th Sunday of Easter** *(Sunday after Ascension Day)*	*W*	[Ezekiel 36.24–28] Acts 1.6–14 Psalm 68.1–10, 32–end [*or* 68.1–10] 1 Peter 4.12–14; 5.6–11 John 17.1–11	Psalm 104.26–35 Isaiah 65.17–end Revelation 21.1–8	Psalm 47 2 Samuel 23.1–5 Ephesians 1.15–end *HC Mark 16.14–end*	*DP* 104

			Holy Communion	Office	2nd Office or Alt HC	Psalmody
Monday	**13 May**	*W*	Acts 19.1–8 Psalm 68.1–6 John 16.29–end	Joshua 1.1–9 1 John 3.11–18	Exodus 10.12–end 2 Timothy 1.1–7 *HC Ps 37.12–17; Luke 6.27–38* **Num 27.15–end; 1 Cor 3*	*MP* 18.1–32, 117 *EP* 122, 125, 126 *DP* 120, 121

or: 1st EP of Matthias: Psalm 147; Isaiah 22.15–22; Philippians 3.13*b*—4.1

			Principal Service	3rd Service	2nd Service	Psalmody
Tuesday	**14 May** Matthias the Apostle	*R*	Isaiah 22.15–end *or* Acts 1.15–end Psalm 15 Acts 1.15–end *or* 1 Corinthians 4.1–7 John 15.9–17	1 Samuel 2.27–35 Acts 2.37–end	1 Samuel 16.1–13*a* Matthew 7.15–27	*MP* 16, 147.1–12 *EP* 80 *DP* 80

			Holy Communion	Office	2nd Office or Alt HC	Psalmody
Wednesday	**15 May**	*W*	Acts 20.28–end Psalm 68.27–28, 32–end John 17.11–19	Isaiah 4.2–end 1 John 4.1–6	Exodus 12.1–14 2 Timothy 2.1–13 *HC Ps 91.1–6; Luke 7.1–17* **1 Kings 18.1–18; Matt 3.13–end*	*MP* 29, 148 *EP* 123, 127, 128, 131 *DP* 124, 125
Thursday	**16 May** *Caroline Chisholm, social reformer*	*W*	Acts 22.30; 23.6–11 Psalm 16.1–2, 6–end John 17.20–end	Zechariah 4 1 John 4.7–end	Exodus 12.21–32 2 Timothy 2.14–end *HC Ps 40.15–end; Luke 7.18–35* **Ezek 11.14–20; Matt 9.35—10.20*	*MP* 144, 146 *EP* 124, 129, 130 *DP* 126, 127
Friday	**17 May**	*W*	Acts 25.13–21 Psalm 103.1–2, 11–12, 19–20 John 21.15–19	Jeremiah 31.27–34 1 John 5.1–12	Exodus 13.17—14.4 2 Timothy 3 *HC Ps 40.10–14; Luke 7.36–end* **Ezek 36.22–28; Matt 12.22–32*	*MP* 46, 76, 147.13–end *EP* 132, 134 *DP* 128, 129
Saturday	**18 May**	*W*	Acts 28.16–20, 30–end Psalm 11.4–end John 21.20–25	Ezekiel 36.22–27 1 John 5.13–end	Exodus 14.5–end 2 Timothy 4.1–8 *HC Ps 111.7–10; Luke 8.1–15* **Micah 3.1–8; Eph 6.10–20*	*MP* 48, 87, 147.1–12 *EP* 48 *DP* 48

1st EP of Pentecost: Deuteronomy 16.9–15; John 15.26—16.15

			Principal Service	3rd Service	2nd Service	Psalmody
Sunday	**19 May** **Pentecost** *Whit Sunday*	*R*	Acts 2.1–21 *or* Numbers 11.24–30 Psalm 104.26–36, 37*b* [*or* 26–37] 1 Corinthians 12.3*b*–13 *or* Acts 2.1–21 John 20.19–23 *or* John 7.37–39	Genesis 11.1–9 Acts 10.34–end	Joel 2.21–end Acts 2.14–21 [22–38] *HC Luke 24.44–end*	*MP* 87 *EP* 67, 133 *DP* 150

			Holy Communion	Office	2nd Office or Alt HC	Psalmody	Alt Pss
Monday	**20 May** Alcuin of York, deacon, abbot (*see* p.67); Ordinary Time resumes today DEL week 7	*Gw*	James 3.13–end Psalm 19.7–end Mark 9.14–29	Proverbs 1.20–end Luke 12.49–end	Proverbs 22.1–16 Ephesians 1 *HC Ps 119.73–80; Mark 11.20–26*	*MP* 119.1–16 *EP* 119.17–32 *DP* 119.17–24	23 25
Tuesday	**21 May** *Helena, protector of the Holy Places*	*G*	James 4.1–10 Psalm 55.6–8, 25 Mark 9.30–37	Proverbs 3.11–20 Luke 13.1–9	Proverbs 30.1–9 Ephesians 2.11–end *HC Ps 119.89–96; Mark 11.27–end*	*MP* 119.33–45 *EP* 119.46–64 *DP* 14	26 27
Wednesday	**22 May**	*G*	James 4.13–end Psalm 49.1–6, 16–18 Mark 9.38–40	Proverbs 4 Luke 13.10–17	Ecclesiastes 1.1–11 Ephesians 3 *HC Ps 19.7–11; Mark 12.1–12*	*MP* 119.65–80 *EP* 119.81–96 *DP* 15	28 29
Thursday	**23 May**	*G*	James 5.1–6 Psalm 49.12–19 Mark 9.41–end	Proverbs 6.1–19 Luke 13.18–30	Ecclesiastes 2.1–11 Ephesians 4 *HC Ps 37.16–19; Mark 12.13–17*	*MP* 119.97–112 *EP* 119.113–128 *DP* 16	30 31
Friday	**24 May** John and Charles Wesley, evangelists, hymn writers (*see* p.66)	*Gw*	James 5.9–12 Psalm 103.1–4, 8–13 Mark 10.1–12	Proverbs 7 Luke 13.31–end	Ecclesiastes 2.12–17 Ephesians 5.1–20 *HC Ps 37.27–32; Mark 12.18–27*	*MP* 119.129–144 *EP* 119.145–160 *DP* 17	32 71
Saturday	**25 May** Venerable Bede, monk (*see* p.67) *Aldhelm, bishop*	*Gw*	James 5.13–end Psalm 141.1–4 Mark 10.13–16	Proverbs 8 Luke 14.1–11 **1st EP of Trinity Sunday:** Exodus 34.1–10; Mark 1.1–13	Ecclesiastes 2.18–26 Ephesians 6 *HC Ps 37.38–end; Mark 12.28–34*	*MP* 119.161–end *EP* 97, 98 *DP* 18.1–32	72

Day	Date	Colour	Principal Service	3rd Service	2nd Service	Psalmody
Sunday	**26 May** Trinity Sunday	*Gold or W*	Isaiah 40.12–17, 27–end Psalm 8 2 Corinthians 13.11–end Matthew 28.16–end	Exodus 3.1–6, 13–15 John 17.1–11	Isaiah 6.1–8 John 16.5–15	*MP* 86.8–13 *EP* 93, 150 *DP* 8
			Holy Communion	**Office**	**2nd Office or Alt HC**	**Psalmody**
Monday	**27 May** DEL week 8	*G*	1 Peter 1.3–9 Psalm 111 Mark 10.17–27	Proverbs 9.1–12 Luke 14.12–24	Ecclesiastes 3.1–15 Colossians 1.1–14 *HC Ps 90.1–4; Mark 12.35–37*	*MP* 1, 2 *EP* 3 [4] *DP* 18.33–end
Tuesday	**28 May** *Lanfranc, monk, archbishop*	*G*	1 Peter 1.10–16 Psalm 98.1–5 Mark 10.28–31	Proverbs 10.1–12 Luke 14.25–end	Ecclesiastes 5.1–7 Colossians 1.15–23 *HC Ps 116.14–end; Mark 12.38–end*	*MP* 5 *EP* 6 *DP* 19
Wednesday	**29 May**	*G*	1 Peter 1.18–end Psalm 147.13–end Mark 10.32–45	Proverbs 15.16–end Luke 15.1–10	Ecclesiastes 5.10–end Colossians 1.24—2.7 *HC Ps 62.5–10; Mark 13.1–13*	*MP* 7 *EP* 8, 9 *DP* 20
				or: 1st EP of Corpus Christi: Psalms 110, 111; Exodus 16.2–15; John 6.22–35		
			Principal Service	**3rd Service**	**2nd Service**	**Psalmody**
Thursday	**30 May** * Day of Thanksgiving for the Institution of Holy Communion (Corpus Christi)	*W [Gw]*	Genesis 14.18–20 Psalm 116.10–end 1 Corinthians 11.23–26 John 6.51–58	Deuteronomy 8.2–16 1 Corinthians 10.1–17	Proverbs 9.1–5 Luke 9.11–17	*MP* 147 *EP* 23, 42, 43 *DP* 23
	** Alternatively, this may be kept more simply as a lesser festival.*					
Or: **Thursday**	**30 May** *If Corpus Christi is not celebrated* Josephine Butler, social reformer (see p.68) *Joan of Arc, visionary; Apolo Kivebulaya, priest, evangelist*	*Gw*	1 Peter 2.2–5, 9–12 Psalm 100 Mark 10.46–end	Proverbs 17.1–17 Luke 15.1–2, 11–end	Ecclesiastes 7.1–13 Colossians 2.8–15 *HC Ps 63.1–5; Mark 13.14–23*	*MP* 10 *EP* 11, 12 *DP* 21
				or: 1st EP of Visit of the BVM to Elizabeth: Psalm 45; Song of Solomon 2.8–14; Luke 1.26–38		
Friday	**31 May** Visit of the BVM to Elizabeth	*W*	Zephaniah 3.14–18 Psalm 113 Romans 12.9–16 Luke 1.39–49 [50–56]	1 Samuel 2.1–10 Mark 3.31–end	Zechariah 2.10–end John 3.25–30	*MP* 85, 150 *EP* 122, 127, 128 *DP* 122
			Holy Communion	**Office**	**2nd Office or Alt HC**	**Psalmody**
Saturday	**1 June** Justin, martyr (see p.65)	*Gr*	Jude vv 17, 20–end Psalm 63.1–6 Mark 11.27–end	Proverbs 25.15–end Luke 16.10–18	Ecclesiastes 12 Colossians 3.12–17 *HC Ps 127; Mark 14.1–9*	*MP* 19 *EP* 17 *DP* 23

		Principal Service		3rd Service	2nd Service	Psalmody
Sunday	**2 June** *G* **1st Sunday after Trinity** Proper 4	*Continuous:* Genesis 6.9–22; 7.24; 8.14–19 Psalm 46	*Related:* Deuteronomy 11.18–21, 26–28 Psalm 31.1–5, 19–end [*or* 31.19–end]	Psalm 37.1–18 Deuteronomy 5.1–21 Acts 21.17–39*a*	Psalm 33 [*or* 33.12–22] Ruth 2.1–20*a* Luke 8.4–15	*DP* 120
		Romans 1.16–17; 3.22*b*–28 [29–31] Matthew 7.21–end				

		Holy Communion	Office	2nd Office or Alt HC	Psalmody
Monday	**3 June** *G* *Martyrs of Uganda, 1886 and 1978* DEL week 9	2 Peter 1.2–7 Psalm 91.1–2, 14–end Mark 12.1–12	Ecclesiastes 1 *or* 1 Maccabees 1.1–19 Luke 16.19–end	Genesis 1.1–28 [*or* 1–5, 26–28] John 1.1–18 *HC Ps 104.1–7*	*MP* 22 *EP* 23 [24] *DP* 119.41–48
Tuesday	**4 June** *G* *Petroc, abbot*	2 Peter 3.11–15, 17–18 Psalm 90.12–end Mark 12.13–17	Ecclesiastes 2 *or* 1 Maccabees 1.20–40 Luke 17.1–10	Isaiah 40.1–5 John 1.19–28 *HC Ps 90.13–end*	*MP* 25 *EP* 26, 27 *DP* 26
Wednesday	**5 June** *Gr* Boniface, bishop, martyr (*see* p.65)	2 Timothy 1.1–3, 6–12 Psalm 123 Mark 12.18–27	Ecclesiastes 3.1–15 *or* 1 Maccabees 1.41–end Luke 17.11–19	Isaiah 53.1–9 John 1.29–34 *HC Ps 130*	*MP* 28, 29 *EP* 30 *DP* 27
Thursday	**6 June** *G* *Ini Kopuria*	2 Timothy 2.8–15 Psalm 25.4–12 Mark 12.28–34	Ecclesiastes 3.16—4.3 *or* 1 Maccabees 2.1–28 Luke 17.20–end	1 Samuel 3.1–10 John 1.35–42 *HC Ps 119.97–100*	*MP* 31.[1–6] 7–end *EP* 32 *DP* 28
Friday	**7 June** *G*	2 Timothy 3.10–end Psalm 119.161–168 Mark 12.35–37	Ecclesiastes 5 *or* 1 Maccabees 2.29–48 Luke 18.1–8	Genesis 28.10–17 John 1.43–end *HC Ps 33.1–6*	*MP* 33 *EP* 34 *DP* 29
Saturday	**8 June** *Gw* Thomas Ken, bishop, nonjuror, hymn writer (*see* p.67)	2 Timothy 4.1–8 Psalm 71.7–16 Mark 12.38–end	Ecclesiastes 6 *or* 1 Maccabees 2.49–end Luke 18.9–14	Exodus 33.12–end John 2.1–11 *HC Ps 18.6–11*	*MP* 35 *EP* 36 *DP* 30

		Principal Service	3rd Service	2nd Service	Psalmody
Sunday	**9 June** *G* **2nd Sunday after Trinity** Proper 5	*Continuous:* Genesis 12.1–9 Psalm 33.1–12 *Related:* Hosea 5.15—6.6 Psalm 50.7–15 Romans 4.13–end Matthew 9.9–13, 18–26	Psalm 38 Deuteronomy 6.10–end Acts 22.22—23.11	Psalms [39] 41 1 Samuel 18.1–16 Luke 8.41–end	*DP* 31

		Holy Communion	Office	2nd Office or Alt HC	Psalmody
Monday	**10 June** *G* DEL week 10	1 Kings 17.1–6 Psalm 121 Matthew 5.1–12	Ecclesiastes 7.1–14 *or* 1 Maccabees 3.1–26 Luke 18.15–30	Deuteronomy 16.1–6 John 2.12–22 *HC Ps 66.7–12*	*MP* 37.1–22 *EP* 37.23–end *DP* 119.49–56
			or: 1st EP of Barnabas: Psalms 1, 15; Isaiah 42.5–12; Acts 14.8–end		

		Principal Service	3rd Service	2nd Service	Psalmody
Tuesday	**11 June** *R* Barnabas the Apostle	Job 29.11–16 *or* Acts 11.19–end Psalm 112 Acts 11.19–end *or* Galatians 2.1–10 John 15.12–17	Jeremiah 9.23–24 Acts 4.32–end	Ecclesiastes 12.9–end *or* Tobit 4.5–11 Acts 9.26–31	*MP* 100, 101, 117 *EP* 147 *DP* 147

		Holy Communion	Office	2nd Office or Alt HC	Psalmody
Wednesday	**12 June** *G*	1 Kings 18.20–39 Psalm 16.1, 6–end Matthew 5.17–19	Ecclesiastes 9.11–end *or* 1 Maccabees 4.1–25 Luke 19.1–10	Numbers 21.4–9 John 3.11–21 *HC Ps 55.1–9*	*MP* 40 *EP* 41 *DP* 33
Thursday	**13 June** *G*	1 Kings 18.41–end Psalm 65.8–end Matthew 5.20–26	Ecclesiastes 11.1–8 *or* 1 Maccabees 4.36–end Luke 19.11–27	Isaiah 1.10–18 John 3.25–end *HC Ps 51.7–13*	*MP* 42, 43 *EP* 44 *DP* 34
Friday	**14 June** *G* *Richard Baxter, Puritan divine*	1 Kings 19.9, 11–16 Psalm 27.8–16 Matthew 5.27–32	Ecclesiastes 11.9—end of 12 *or* 1 Maccabees 9.1–22 Luke 19.28–40	2 Kings 17.29, 34–39 John 4.1–26 *HC Ps 115.3–8*	*MP* 45 *EP* 46, 47 *DP* 35
Saturday	**15 June** *G* *Evelyn Underhill, spiritual writer*	1 Kings 19.19–end Psalm 16.1–7 Matthew 5.33–37	Numbers 3.1–13 Luke 19.41–end	Micah 6.9–end John 4.27–42 *HC Ps 24.1–8*	*MP* 48 *EP* 49 *DP* 36

		Principal Service		3rd Service	2nd Service	Psalmody
Sunday	**16 June** *G* 3rd Sunday after Trinity Proper 6	*Continuous:* Genesis 18.1–15 [*or* 21.1–7] Psalm 116.1, 10–17 [*or* 116.9–17]	*Related:* Exodus 19.2–8*a* Psalm 100	Psalm 45 Deuteronomy 10.12–11.1 Acts 23.12–end	Psalms [42] 43 1 Samuel 21 Luke 11.14–28	*DP* 37
		Romans 5.1–8 Matthew 9.35—10.8 [9–23]				

		Holy Communion	Office	2nd Office or Alt HC	Psalmody
Monday	**17 June** *G* *Samuel and Henrietta Barnett, social reformers* DEL week 11	1 Kings 21.1–16 Psalm 5.1–5 Matthew 5.38–42	Numbers 6.22–end Luke 20.1–8	Proverbs 16.1–20 John 4.43–end *HC Ps 119.65–72*	*MP* 50 *EP* 51 *DP* 119.57–64
Tuesday	**18 June** *G* *Bernard Mizeki, martyr*	1 Kings 21.17–end Psalm 51.1–9 Matthew 5.43–end	Numbers 9.15–end; 10.29–end Luke 20.9–19	Nehemiah 3.1–2; 4.1–6 John 5.2–18 *HC Ps 123*	*MP* 52, 53 *EP* 54, 55 *DP* 38
Wednesday	**19 June** *G* *Sundar Singh, evangelist, teacher of the faith*	2 Kings 2.1, 6–14 Psalm 31.21–end Matthew 6.1–6, 16–18	Numbers 11 Luke 20.19–26	Deuteronomy 5.22–end John 5.19–29 *HC Ps 111.1–6*	*MP* 56 *EP* 57 *DP* 39
Thursday	**20 June** *G*	Ecclesiasticus 48.1–14 *or* Isaiah 63.7–9 Psalm 97.1–8 Matthew 6.7–15	Numbers 12 Luke 20.27–40	Exodus 16.1–16 John 6.1–21 *HC Ps 78.23–29*	*MP* [58] 59 *EP* 60 *DP* 40
Friday	**21 June** *G*	2 Kings 11.1–4, 9–18, 20 Psalm 132.1–5, 11–13 Matthew 6.19–23	Numbers 13.1–3, 21—14.10 Luke 20.41—21.4	Exodus 16.17–35 John 6.25–40 *HC Ps 78.32–37*	*MP* 61 *EP* 62 *DP* 41
Saturday	**22 June** *Gr* Alban, martyr (see p.65)	2 Chronicles 24.17–25 Psalm 89.25–33 Matthew 6.24–end	Numbers 14.10–end Luke 21.5–19	Exodus 17.1–7 John 6.41–58 *HC Ps 105.37–42*	*MP* [63] 64 *EP* 65 *DP* 42

		Principal Service		3rd Service	2nd Service	Psalmody
Sunday	**23 June** *G* **4th Sunday after Trinity** Proper 7	*Continuous:* Genesis 21.8–21 Psalm 86.1–10, 16–end [*or* 86.1–10]	*Related:* Jeremiah 20.7–13 Psalm 69.8–11 [12–17] 18–20 [*or* 69.14–20]	Psalm 49 Deuteronomy 11.1–15 Acts 27.1–12	Psalms 46 [48] 1 Samuel 24.1–17 Luke 14.12–24	*DP* 43
		Romans 6.1*b*–11 Matthew 10.24–39		*Or:* 1st EP of Birth of John the Baptist: Psalm 71; Judges 13.2–7, 24–end; Luke 1.5–25		
Monday	**24 June** *W* Birth of John the Baptist	Isaiah 40.1–11 Psalm 85.7–13 Acts 13.14*b*–26 *or* Gal 3.23–end Luke 1.57–66, 80		Ecclesiasticus 48.1–10 *or* Malachi 3.1–6 Luke 3.1–17	Malachi 4 Matthew 11.2–19	*MP* 50, 149 *EP* 80, 82 *DP* 80

		Holy Communion	Office	2nd Office or Alt HC	Psalmody
Tuesday	**25 June** *G* DEL week 12	2 Kings 19.9–11, 14–21*a*, 31–36 Psalm 48.1–2, 8–end Matthew 7.6, 12–14	Numbers 16.20–35 Luke 21.29–36	Isaiah 58.1–8 John 8.12–20 *HC Ps 147.7–12*	*MP* 69 *EP* 70, 71 *DP* 44
Wednesday	**26 June** *G* Ember Day (see p.6)	2 Kings 22.8–13; 23.1–3 Psalm 119.33–40 Matthew 7.15–20	Numbers 16.36–end Luke 21.37—22.13	Ecclesiasticus 42.15–end *or* Deuteronomy 28.58–end John 8.31–47 *HC Ps 139.6–11*	*MP* 72 *EP* 73 *DP* 45
Thursday	**27 June** *G* *Cyril, bishop, teacher of the faith*	2 Kings 24.8–17 Psalm 79. 1–9, 12 Matthew 7.21–end	Numbers 17.1–11 Luke 22.14–23	Genesis 15.1–15 John 8.48–end *HC Ps 113.5–end*	*MP* 74 *EP* 75, 76 *DP* 46
Friday	**28 June** *Gw* Irenæus, bishop, teacher of the faith (see p.66) Ember Day	2 Kings 25.1–12 Psalm 137.1–6 Matthew 8.1–4	Numbers 20 Luke 22.24–30	Ezekiel 18.1–4, 19–23 John 9.1–12 *HC Ps 119.109–112*	*MP* 77 *EP* 78.1–20 *DP* 47
			or: 1st EP of Peter and Paul [*Peter alone]: Psalms 66, 67; Ezekiel 3.4–11; Galatians 1.13—2.8 [*Acts 9.32–end]		

		Principal Service		3rd Service	2nd Service	Psalmody
Saturday	**29 June** *R* Peter and Paul, apostles *or* Peter the Apostle Ember Day	*Peter & Paul:* Zechariah 4.1–6*a*, 10*b*–end *or* Acts 12.1–11 Psalm 125 Acts 12.1–11 *or* 2 Timothy 4.6–8, 17–18 Matthew 16.13–19	*Peter alone:* Ezekiel 3.22–end *or* Acts 12.1–11 Psalm 125 Acts 12.1–11 *or* 1 Peter 2.19–end Matthew 16.13–19	Isaiah 49.1–6 Acts 11.1–18	Ezekiel 34.11–16 John 21.15–22	*MP* 71, 113 *EP* 124, 138 *DP* 124

			Principal Service		3rd Service	2nd Service	Psalmody
Sunday	**30 June** **5th Sunday after Trinity** Proper 8	*G*	*Continuous:* Genesis 22.1–14 Psalm 13	*Related:* Jeremiah 28.5–9 Psalm 89.1–4, 15–18 [*or* 89.8–18]	Psalms 52, 53 Deuteronomy 15.1–11 Acts 27.[13–32] 33–end	Psalm 50 [*or* 50.1–15] 1 Samuel 28.3–19 Luke 17.20–end	*DP* 49
			Romans 6.12–end Matthew 10.40–end				

			Holy Communion	Office	2nd Office or Alt HC	Psalmody
Monday	**1 July** *Henry, John and Henry Venn, priests, evangelical divines* DEL week 13	*G*	Amos 2.6–10, 13–end Psalm 50.16–23 Matthew 8.18–22	Numbers 22.1–21 Luke 22.39–51	Zechariah 10.6–end John 10.1–10 *HC Ps 77.16–end*	*MP* 79 *EP* 80 *DP* 119.73–80
Tuesday	**2 July**	*G*	Amos 3.1–8; 4.11–12 Psalm 5.8–end Matthew 8.23–27	Numbers 22.21–38 Luke 22.52–62	Ezekiel 34.11–16 John 10.11–18 *HC Ps 80.1–8*	*MP* 81 *EP* 82, 83 *DP* 50
				or: 1st EP of Thomas: Psalm 27; Isaiah 35; Hebrews 10.35—11.1		

			Principal Service	3rd Service	2nd Service	Psalmody
Wednesday	**3 July** Thomas the Apostle	*R*	Habakkuk 2.1–4 Psalm 31.1–6 Ephesians 2.19–end John 20.24–29	2 Samuel 15.17–21 *or* Ecclesiasticus 2 John 11.1–16	Job 42.1–6 1 Peter 1.3–12	*MP* 92, 146 *EP* 139 *DP* 139

			Holy Communion	Office	2nd Office or Alt HC	Psalmody
Thursday	**4 July**	*G*	Amos 7.10–end Psalm 19.7–10 Matthew 9.1–8	Numbers 23.11–26 Luke 23.1–12	Jeremiah 31.1–14 John 11.17–27 *HC Ps 149.1–4*	*MP* 87, 88 *EP* 89.1–18 *DP* 52
Friday	**5 July**	*G*	Amos 8.4–6, 9–12 Psalm 119.1–8 Matthew 9.9–13	Numbers 24.1–13 Luke 23.13–25	Ezekiel 37.1–14 John 11.28–44 *HC Ps 119.169–end*	*MP* 89.19–37 *EP* 89.38–end *DP* 53
Saturday	**6 July** *Thomas More, scholar, and John Fisher, bishop, martyrs*	*G*	Amos 9.11–end Psalm 85.8–end Matthew 9.14–17	Numbers 24.12–end Luke 23.26–31	Isaiah 28.9–16 John 11.45–end *HC Ps 14*	*MP* 90 *EP* [91] 92 *DP* 54

			Principal Service		3rd Service	2nd Service	Psalmody
Sunday	**7 July** **6th Sunday after Trinity** Proper 9	*G*	*Continuous:* Genesis 24.34–38, 42–49, 58–end Psalm 45.10–17 *or* Song of Sol 2.8–13 Romans 7.15–25*a* Matthew 11.16–19, 25–end	*Related:* Zechariah 9.9–12 Psalm 145.8–15	Psalm 55.1–15, 18–22 Deuteronomy 24.10–end Acts 28.1–16	Psalm 56 [57] 2 Samuel 2.1–11; 3.1 Luke 18.31—19.10	*DP* 55

			Holy Communion	Office	2nd Office or Alt HC	Psalmody
Monday	**8 July** DEL week 14	*G*	Hosea 2.16–18, 21–22 Psalm 145.2–9 Matthew 9.18–26	Numbers 27.12–end Luke 23.32–43	Deuteronomy 15.1–11 John 12.1–8 *HC Ps 94.8–11*	*MP* 93, 94 *EP* [96] 97 *DP* 119.81–88
Tuesday	**9 July**	*G*	Hosea 8.4–7, 11–13 Psalm 103.8–12 Matthew 9.32–end	Numbers 32.1–27 Luke 23.44–56*a*	Zechariah 9.9–12 John 12.12–19 *HC Ps 72.1–8*	MP [95] 98 *EP* 99 *DP* 56
Wednesday	**10 July**	*G*	Hosea 10.1–3, 7–8, 12 Psalm 115.3–10 Matthew 10.1–7	Numbers 35 Luke 23.56*b*—24.12	2 Esdras 9.[15–25] 26–33 *or* Zechariah 8.14–end John 12.20–26 *HC Ps 119.113–114*	*MP* [100] 101 *EP* 102 *DP* 57
Thursday	**11 July** Benedict, abbot (*see* p.67)	*Gw*	Hosea 11.1, 3–4, 8–9 Psalm 105.1–7 Matthew 10.7–15	Deuteronomy 1.1–18 Luke 24.13–35	2 Esdras 2.42–end *or* Ezekiel 37.24–end John 12.27–36*a* *HC Ps 78.67–end*	*MP* [103], *or* 105.1–22 *EP* [104], *or* 105.23–end *DP* 58
Friday	**12 July**	*G*	Hosea 14.2–end Psalm 80.1–7 Matthew 10.16–23	Deuteronomy 3.18–28 Luke 24.36–end	Ecclesiasticus 32.14–20, 24 *or* Isaiah 6.[1–5] 6–13*a* John 12.37–50 *HC Ps 62.1–7*	*MP* 106.1–23 *EP* 106.24–end *DP* 59
Saturday	**13 July**	*G*	Isaiah 6.1–8 Psalm 51.1–7 Matthew 10.24–33	Deuteronomy 31.7–13; ch 34 Romans 1.1–15	Lamentations 3.1–6, 19–26 John 13.1–20 *HC Ps 16.7–end*	*MP* 107.1–22 *EP* 107.23–end *DP* 60

		Principal Service		3rd Service	2nd Service	Psalmody
Sunday	**14 July** *G* **7th Sunday after Trinity** Proper 10	*Continuous:* Genesis 25.19–end Psalm 119.105–112	*Related:* Isaiah 55.10–13 Psalm 65.[1–7] 8–end [*or* 65.8–end]	Psalms 64, 65 Deuteronomy 28.1–14 Acts 28.17–end	Psalms 60 [63] 2 Samuel 7.18–end Luke 19.41—20.8	*DP* 61
		Romans 8.1–11 Matthew 13.1–9, 18–23				

		Holy Communion	Office	2nd Office or Alt HC	Psalmody	Alt Pss
Monday	**15 July** *Gw* Swithun, bishop (see p.67) *Bonaventure, friar, bishop, teacher of the faith* DEL week 15	Isaiah 1.11–17 Psalm 50.7–15 Matthew 10.34—11.1	Joshua 1 Romans 1.16–25 [26–27]	Leviticus 19.1, 17–18 John 13.21–end *HC Ps 15*	*MP* 108 [109] *EP* 110, 111 *DP* 119.89–96	
Tuesday	**16 July** *G* *Osmund, bishop*	Isaiah 7.1–9 Psalm 48.1–7 Matthew 11.20–24	Joshua 2 Romans 1.28—2.11	Deuteronomy 31.1–13 John 14.1–7 *HC Ps 119.33–40*	*MP* 112 *EP* 113 *DP* 62	
Wednesday	**17 July** *G*	Isaiah 10.5–7, 13–16 Psalm 94.5–11 Matthew 11.25–27	Joshua 3.1–13 Romans 2.12–24	Wisdom 6.12–19 *or* Proverbs 8.12–21 John 14.8–24 *HC Ps 111.7–end*	*MP* 114 *EP* 115 *DP* 63	
Thursday	**18 July** *G* *Elizabeth Ferard, deaconess*	Isaiah 26.7–9, 16–19 Psalm 102.14–21 Matthew 11.28–end	Joshua 3.14—4.7 Romans 2.25—3.8	Exodus 19.1–6 John 14.25–end *HC Ps 135.1–4*	*MP* 116, 117 *EP* 118 *DP* 64	
Friday	**19 July** *Gw* Gregory, bishop, and Macrina, deaconess, teachers of the faith (see p.66)	Isaiah 38.1–6, 21–22, 7–8 [*sic*] *Canticle:* Isaiah 38.10–16 *or* Psalm 32.1–8 Matthew 12.1–8	Joshua 4.19—5.1 [2–9] 10–15 Romans 3.9–20	Isaiah 5.1–10 John 15.1–11 *HC Ps 80.9–16*	*MP* 119.1–16 *EP* 119.17–32 *DP* 65	23 25
Saturday	**20 July** *G* *Margaret of Antioch, martyr; Bartolomé de las Casas, missionary*	Micah 2.1–5 Psalm 10.1–5*a*, 12 Matthew 12.14–21	Joshua 6 Romans 3.21–end	Deuteronomy 7.6–11 John 15.12–17 *HC Ps 85.1–4*	*MP* 119.33–48 *EP* 119.49–64 *DP* 66	26 27

		Principal Service		3rd Service	2nd Service	Psalmody
Sunday	**21 July** *G* **8th Sunday after Trinity** Proper 11	*Continuous:* Genesis 28.10–19*a* Psalm 139.1–11, 23–end [*or* 139.1–11]	*Related:* Wisdom 12.13, 16–19 *or* Isaiah 44.6–8 Psalm 86.11–end	Psalm 71 Deuteronomy 30.1–10 1 Peter 3.8–18	Psalms 67 [70] 1 Kings 2.10–12; 3.16–end Acts 4.1–22 *HC Mark 6.30–34, 53–end*	*DP* 67
		Romans 8.12–25 Matthew 13.24–30, 36–43		*or:* 1st EP of Mary Magdalene: Psalm 139; Isaiah 25.1–9; 2 Corinthians 1.3–7		
Monday	**22 July** *W* Mary Magdalene	Song of Solomon 3.1–4 Psalm 42.1–10 2 Corinthians 5.14–17 John 20.1–2, 11–18		1 Samuel 16.14–end Luke 8.1–3	Zephaniah 3.14–end Mark 15.40—16.7 *DP* 63	*MP* 30, 32, 150 *EP* 63

		Holy Communion	Office	2nd Office or Alt HC	Psalmody / Alt Pss
Tuesday	**23 July** *G* *Bridget of Sweden, abbess* DEL week 16	Micah 7.14–15, 15, 18–20 Psalm 85.1–7 Matthew 12.46–end	Joshua 8.1–22 Romans 4.13–end	Job 40.1–14 John 16.16–24 *HC Ps 119.25–32*	*MP* 119.97–112 / 30 *EP* 119.113–128 / 31 *DP* 68
Wednesday	**24 July** *G*	Jeremiah 1.1, 4–10 Psalm 70 Matthew 13.1–9	Joshua 8.30–end Romans 5.1–11	Isaiah 63.7–14 John 16.25–end *HC Ps 145.1–5*	*MP* 119.129–144 / 32 *EP* 119.145–160 / 71 *DP* 69
			or: 1st EP of James the Apostle: Psalm 144; Deuteronomy 30.11–end; Mark 5.21–end		

		Principal Service	3rd Service	2nd Service	Psalmody
Thursday	**25 July** *R* James the Apostle	Jeremiah 45.1–5 *or* Acts 11.27—12.2 Psalm 126 Acts 11.27—12.2 *or* 2 Corinthians 4.7–15 Matthew 20.20–end	2 Kings 1.9–15 Luke 9.46–56	Jeremiah 26.1–15 Mark 1.14–20	*MP* 7, 29, 117 *EP* 94 *DP* 94

		Holy Communion	Office	2nd Office or Alt HC	Psalmody
Friday	**26 July** *Gw* Anne and Joachim, parents of the BVM	Jeremiah 3.14–17 Psalm 23 *or Canticle:* Jeremiah 31.10–13 Matthew 3.18–23	Joshua 9.22—10.15 Romans 6.1–11	Isaiah 56.1–8 John 17.20–end *HC Ps 34.11–14*	*MP* 122, 123 *EP* 124, 125 *DP* 71
		Lesser festival eucharistic lectionary: Zephaniah 3.14–17; Psalm 127; Romans 8.28–30; Matthew 13.16–17			
Saturday	**27 July** *G* *Brooke Foss Westcott, bishop, teacher of the faith*	Jeremiah 7.1–11 Psalm 84.1–6 Matthew 13.24–30	Joshua 23.1—24.13 Romans 6.12–end	Joshua 1.1–9 John 18.1–14 *HC Ps 27.1–8*	*MP* 126, 127 *EP* 128, 129 *DP* 72

			Principal Service		3rd Service	2nd Service	Psalmody
Sunday	**28 July** **9th Sunday after Trinity** Proper 12	*G*	*Continuous:* Genesis 29.15–28 Psalm 105.1–11, 45*b* [*or* 105.1–11]; *or* 128 Romans 8.26–end Matthew 13.31–33, 44–52	*Related:* 1 Kings 3.5–12 Psalm 119.129–136	Psalm 77 Song of Solomon 2 *or* 1 Maccabees 2.[1–14] 15–22 1 Peter 4.7–14	Psalms 75 [76] 1 Kings 6.11–14, 23–end Acts 12.1–17 *HC John 6.1–21*	*DP* 73

			Holy Communion	Office	2nd Office or Alt HC	Psalmody
Monday	**29 July** Mary, Martha and Lazarus, companions of Our Lord DEL week 17	*Gw*	Jeremiah 13.1–11 Psalm 82 *or* Deuteronomy 32.18–21 Matthew 13.31–35	Joshua 24.14–end Romans 7.1–12	Joshua 4.1–11 John 18.15–27 *HC Ps 114*	*MP* 130, 131, 146 *EP* 132 *DP* 119.105–112
			Lesser festival eucharistic lectionary: Isaiah 25.6–9; Psalm 49.5–10, 16; Hebrews 2.10–15; John 12.1–8			
Tuesday	**30 July** William Wilberforce, social reformer (see p.68)	*Gw*	Jeremiah 14.17–end Psalm 79.8–end Matthew 13.36–43	Judges 2 Romans 7.13–end	Joshua 6.1–21 John 18.28–end *HC Ps 35.23–end*	*MP* 133 [134] 147.1–12 *EP* 135 *DP* 74
Wednesday	**31 July** *Ignatius of Loyola*	*G*	Jeremiah 15.10, 16–end Psalm 59.1–4, 18–end Matthew 13.44–46	Judges 3.12–30 Romans 8.1–11	Joshua 23 John 19.1–7 *HC Ps 54*	*MP* 136, 147.13–end *EP* 137, 138 *DP* 75
Thursday	**1 August**	*G*	Jeremiah 18.1–6 Psalm 146.1–5 Matthew 13.47–53	Judges 4.4–23 Romans 8.12–17	Joshua 24 John 19.8–16*a* *HC Ps 2.7–11a*	*MP* 139, 148 *EP* 140 *DP* 76
Friday	**2 August**	*G*	Jeremiah 26.1–9 Psalm 69.4–10 Matthew 13.54–end	Judges 5 Romans 8.18–25	1 Samuel 8 John 19.16*b*–25*a* *HC Ps 28.7–end*	*MP* 141, 149 *EP* 142, 143 *DP* 77
Saturday	**3 August**	*G*	Jeremiah 26.11–16, 24 Psalm 69.14–20 Matthew 14.1–12	Judges 6.1–24 Romans 8.26–30	Judges 13.2–end John 19.25*b*–30 *HC Ps 116.10–end*	*MP* 144, 150 *EP* 145 *DP* 78.1–38

		Principal Service		3rd Service	2nd Service	Psalmody
Sunday	**4 August** *G* **10th Sunday after Trinity** Proper 13	*Continuous:* Genesis 32.22–31 Psalm 17.1–7, 16 [*or* 17.1–7]	*Related:* Isaiah 55.1–5 Psalm 145.8–9, 15–end [*or* 145.15–22]	Psalm 85 Song of Solomon 5.2–end *or* 1 Maccabees 3.1–12 2 Peter 1.1–15	Psalm 80 [*or* 80.1–8] 1 Kings 10.1–13 Acts 13.1–13 *HC John 6.24–35*	*DP* 78.40–end
		Romans 9.1–5 Matthew 14.13–21				

		Holy Communion	Office	2nd Office or Alt HC	Psalmody
Monday	**5 August** *Gr* Oswald, king, martyr (see p.65) DEL week 18	Jeremiah 28 Psalm 119.89–96 Matthew 14.13–21 *or* 14.22–end	Judges 6.25–end Romans 8.31–end	Judges 14 John 19.31–end *HC Ps 129*	*MP* 1, 2 *EP* 3 [4] *DP* 119.113–120
			or: 1st EP of the Transfiguration: Psalms 99, 110; Exodus 24.12–end; John 12.27–36*a*		

		Principal Service	3rd Service	2nd Service	Psalmody
Tuesday	**6 August** *Gold or W* Transfiguration of Our Lord	Daniel 7.9–10, 13–14 Psalm 97 2 Peter 1.16–19 Luke 9.28–36	Ecclesiasticus 48.1–10 *or* 1 Kings 19.1–16 1 John 3.1–3	Exodus 34.29–end 2 Corinthians 3	*MP* 27, 150 *EP* 72 *DP* 72

		Holy Communion	Office	2nd Office or Alt HC	Psalmody
Wednesday	**7 August** *G* *John Mason Neale, priest, hymn writer*	Jeremiah 31.1–7 Psalm 121 Matthew 15.21–28	Judges 7.19—8.12 Romans 9.19–end	Judges 16.1–16 John 20.11–18 *HC Ps 86.1–7*	*MP* 7 *EP* 8, 9 *DP* 80
Thursday	**8 August** *Gw* Dominic, priest (see p.67)	Jeremiah 31.31–34 Psalm 51.11–18 Matthew 16.13–23	Judges 8.22–end Romans 10.1–13	Judges 16.17–end John 20.19–23 *HC Ps 140.9–end*	*MP* 10 *EP* 11, 12 *DP* 81
Friday	**9 August** *Gw* Mary Sumner (see p.68)	Nahum 2.1, 3; 3.1–3, 6–7 Psalm 137.1–6 *or* Deuteronomy 32.35–36, 39, 41 Matthew 16.24–28	Judges 9.1–21 Romans 10.14–end	1 Chronicles 13 John 20.24–end *HC Ps 135.1–4*	*MP* 13, 14 *EP* 15, 16 *DP* 82
Saturday	**10 August** *Gr* Laurence, deacon, martyr (see p.65)	Habakkuk 1.12—2.4 Psalm 9.7–11 Matthew 17.14–20	Judges 9.22–25, 50–end Romans 11.1–12	1 Chronicles 16.8–36 John 21 *HC Ps 117*	*MP* 19 *EP* 17 *DP* 83* [*or* 8]

*See page 4, under Psalms.

		Principal Service		3rd Service	2nd Service	Psalmody
Sunday	**11 August** *G* **11th Sunday after Trinity** Proper 14	*Continuous:* Genesis 37.1–4, 12–28 Psalm 105.1–6, 16–22, 45*b* [*or* 105.1–10]	*Related:* 1 Kings 19.9–18 Psalm 85.8–end	Psalm 88 Song of Solomon 8.5–7 *or* 1 Maccabees 14.4–15 2 Peter 3.8–13	Psalm 86 1 Kings 11.41—12.20 Acts 14.8–20 *HC John 6.35, 41–51*	*DP* 84
		Romans 10.5–15 Matthew 14.22–33				

		Holy Communion	Office	2nd Office or Alt HC	Psalmody
Monday	**12 August** *G* DEL week 19	Ezekiel 1.2–5, 24–end Psalm 148.1–4, 12–13*a* Matthew 17.22–end	Judges 11.1–11, 29—12.7 Romans 11.13–24	1 Chronicles 17.1–15 1 Corinthians 1.18–end *HC Ps 132.11–end; Luke 8.16–25*	*MP* 18.1–24 *EP* 18.25–end *DP* 119.121–128
Tuesday	**13 August** *Gw* Jeremy Taylor, bishop, teacher of the faith (*see* p.66) *Florence Nightingale, Octavia Hill, social reformers*	Ezekiel 2.8—3.4 Psalm 119.65–72 Matthew 18.1–5, 10, 12–14	Judges 13.1–14 Romans 11.25–36	1 Chronicles 28.2–10 1 Corinthians 2 *HC Ps 121; Luke 8.26–39*	*MP* 20 *EP* 21 *DP* 85
Wednesday	**14 August** *G* *Maximilian Kolbe, friar, martyr*	Ezekiel 9.1–7; 10.18–22 Psalm 113 Matthew 18.15–20	Judges 13.15–24 Romans 12.1–8	1 Chronicles 28.11–end 1 Corinthians 3 *HC Ps 122; Luke 8.40–end*	*MP* 22 *EP* 23 [24] *DP* 86
			or: 1st EP of the Blessed Virgin Mary: Psalm 72; Proverbs 8.22–31; John 19.23–27		

		Principal Service	3rd Service	2nd Service	Psalmody
Thursday	**15 August** *W* The Blessed Virgin Mary	Isaiah 61.10–end *or* Revelation 11.19—12.6, 10 Psalm 45.10–end Galatians 4.4–7 Luke 1.46–55	Isaiah 7.10–15 Luke 11.27–28	Song of Solomon 2.1–7 Acts 1.6–14	*MP* 98, 138, 147.1–12 *EP* 132 *DP* 132

		Holy Communion	Office	2nd Office or Alt HC	Psalmody
Friday	**16 August** *G*	Ezekiel 16.1–15, 60–end Psalm 118.14–18 Matthew 19.3–12	Judges 14.20—16.3 Romans 13.1–7	1 Chronicles 29.10–20 1 Corinthians 6.1–11 *HC Ps 77.11–15; Luke 9.18–27*	*MP* 28, 29 *EP* 30 *DP* 88
Saturday	**17 August** *G*	Ezekiel 18.1–10, 13, 30, 32 Psalm 51.1–3, 15–17 Matthew 19.13–15	Judges 16.4–end Romans 13.8–end	1 Chronicles 29.21–30 1 Corinthians 8 *HC Ps 77.11–15; Luke 9.28–36*	*MP* 31.[1–6] 7–end *EP* 32 *DP* 89

		Principal Service		3rd Service	2nd Service	Psalmody
Sunday	**18 August** *G* **12th Sunday after Trinity** Proper 15	*Continuous:* Genesis 45.1–15 Psalm 133	*Related:* Isaiah 56.1, 6–8 Psalm 67	Psalm 92 Jonah 1 *or* Ecclesiasticus 3.1–15 2 Peter 3.14–end	Psalm 90 [*or* 90.1–12] 2 Kings 4.1–37 Acts 16.1–15 *HC John 6.51–58*	*DP* 90
		Romans 11.1–2*a*, 29–32 Matthew 15.[10–20] 21–28				

		Holy Communion	Office	2nd Office or Alt HC	Psalmody
Monday	**19 August** *G* DEL week 20	Ezekiel 24.15–24 Psalm 78.1–8 Matthew 19.16–22	Judges 17 Romans 14.1–12	2 Chronicles 1 1 Corinthians 9.1–2, 19–end *HC Ps 119.41–48; Luke 9.37–50*	*MP* 33 *EP* 34 *DP* 119.129–136
Tuesday	**20 August** *Gw* Bernard, abbot, teacher of the faith (see p.66) *William and Catherine Booth*	Ezekiel 28.1–10 Psalm 107.1–3, 40, 43 Matthew 19.23–end	Judges 18.1–15 Romans 14.13–end	2 Chronicles 2 1 Corinthians 10.14—11.1 *HC Ps 76.7–end; Luke 9.51–end*	*MP* 35 *EP* 36 *DP* 91
Wednesday	**21 August** *G*	Ezekiel 34.1–11 Psalm 23 Matthew 20.1–16	Judges 18.16–end Romans 15.1–13	2 Chronicles 3 1 Corinthians 11.17–end *HC Ps 93; Luke 10.1–16*	*MP* 37.1–22 *EP* 37.23–end *DP* 92
Thursday	**22 August** *G*	Ezekiel 36.23–28 Psalm 51.7–12 Matthew 22.1–14	Job 1.1—2.10 Romans 15.14–29	2 Chronicles 5.2—6.11 1 Corinthians 12.1–11 *HC Ps 132.7–end; Luke 10.17–24*	*MP* 38 *EP* 39 *DP* 93
Friday	**23 August** *G*	Ezekiel 37.1–14 Psalm 107.1–8 Matthew 22.34–40	Job 2.11—end of 3 Romans 15.30—16.16	2 Chronicles 6.12–end 1 Corinthians 12.12–end *HC Ps 135.15–end; Luke 10.25–37*	*MP* 40 *EP* 41 *DP* 94
			or: 1st EP of Bartholomew the Apostle: Psalm 97; Isaiah 61.1–9; 2 Corinthians 6.1–10		

		Principal Service	3rd Service	2nd Service	Psalmody
Saturday	**24 August** *R* Bartholomew the Apostle	Isaiah 43.8–13 *or* Acts 5.12–16 Psalm 145.1–7 Acts 5.12–16 *or* 1 Corinthians 4.9–15 Luke 22.24–30	Genesis 28.10–17 John 1.43–end	Ecclesiasticus 39.1–10 *or* Deuteronomy 18.15–19 Matthew 10.1–22	*MP* 86, 117 *EP* 91, 116 *DP* 91

		Principal Service		3rd Service	2nd Service	Psalmody
Sunday	**25 August** *G* **13th Sunday after Trinity** Proper 16	*Continuous:* Exodus 1.8—2.10 Psalm 124 Romans 12.1–8 Matthew 16.13–20	*Related:* Isaiah 51.1–6 Psalm 138	Psalm 104.1–25 Jonah 2 *or* Ecclesiasticus 3.17–29 Revelation 1	Psalm 95 2 Kings 6.8–23 Acts 17.15–end *HC John 6.56–69*	*DP* 96

		Holy Communion	Office	2nd Office or Alt HC	Psalmody
Monday	**26 August** *G* DEL week 21	2 Thessalonians 1.1–5, 11–12 Psalm 39.1–9 Matthew 23.13–22	Job [4.1] 5 John 20.1–10	2 Chronicles 30.1–9 Acts 1 *HC Ps 129; Matt 1.18–end*	*MP* 45 *EP* 46, 47 *DP* 119.137–144
Tuesday	**27 August** *Gw* Monica, mother of Augustine of Hippo (see p.68)	2 Thessalonians 2.1–3*a*, 14–17 Psalm 98 Matthew 23.23–26	Job 6.1–21 John 20.11–18	2 Chronicles 34.1–11 Acts 2.1–21 *HC Ps 54; Matt 2.1–12*	*MP* 48 *EP* 49 *DP* 97
Wednesday	**28 August** *Gw* Augustine of Hippo, bishop, teacher of the faith (see p.66)	2 Thessalonians 3.6–10, 16–18 Psalm 128 Matthew 23.27–32	Job [6.1] 7 John 20.19–31	2 Chronicles 34.14–15, 29–end Acts 2.22–41 *HC Ps 68.32–end; Matt 2.13–end*	*MP* 50 *EP* 51 *DP* 98
Thursday	**29 August** *Gr* Beheading of John the Baptist	1 Corinthians 1.1–9 Psalm 145.1–7 Matthew 24.42–end	Job 8 John 21.1–14	Song of Solomon 8.5–7 Acts 2.42—3.10 *HC Ps 127; Matt 3.1–6*	*MP* 52, 53 *EP* 54, 55 *DP* 99
		Lesser festival eucharistic lectionary: Jeremiah 1.4–10; Psalm 11; Hebrews 11.32—12.2; Matthew 14.1–12			
Friday	**30 August** *Gw* John Bunyan, spiritual writer (see p.66)	1 Corinthians 1.17–25 Psalm 33.6–12 Matthew 25.1–13	Job 9 John 21.15–19	Jeremiah 1.4–10 Acts 3.12–26 *HC Ps 119.41–48; Matt 3.7–end*	*MP* 56 *EP* 57 *DP* 100
Saturday	**31 August** *Gw* Aidan, bishop, missionary (see p.67)	1 Corinthians 1.26–end Psalm 33.12–15, 20–end Matthew 25.14–30	Job [9.1] 10 John 21.20–end	Jeremiah 2.4–13 Acts 4.1–22 *HC Ps 60.1–5; Matt 4.1–11*	*MP* [58] 59 *EP* 60 *DP* 101

		Principal Service		3rd Service	2nd Service	Psalmody
Sunday	**1 September** *G* **14th Sunday after Trinity** Proper 17	*Continuous:* Exodus 3.1–15 Psalm 105.1–6, 23–26, 45*b* [*or* 115] Romans 12.9–end Matthew 16.21–end	*Related:* Jeremiah 15.15–end Psalm 26.1–8	Psalm 107.1–32 Jonah 3.1–9 *or* Ecclesiasticus 11.7–28 [*or* 19–28] Revelation 3.14–end	Psalm 105.1–15 2 Kings 6.24–25; 7.3–end Acts 18.1–16 *HC Mark 7.1–8, 14–15, 21–23*	*DP* 102

		Holy Communion	Office	2nd Office or Alt HC	Psalmody
Monday	**2 September** *G* *Martyrs of Papua New Guinea, 1901 and 1942* DEL week 22	1 Corinthians 2.1–5 Psalm 33.12–21 Luke 4.16–30	Job 11 Ephesians 1.1–14	Jeremiah 5.20–end Acts 4.23–end *HC Ps 77.5–10; Matt 4.12–17*	*MP* 61 *EP* 62 *DP* 119.145–152
Tuesday	**3 September** *Gw* Gregory the Great, bishop, teacher of the faith (see p.66)	1 Corinthians 2.10–end Psalm 145.10–17 Luke 4.31–37	Job 12 Ephesians 1.15–end	Jeremiah 7.1–15 Acts 5.1–16 *HC Ps 14; Matt 4.18–end*	*MP* [63] 64 *EP* 65 *DP* 103
Wednesday	**4 September** *G* *Birinus, bishop*	1 Corinthians 3.1–9 Psalm 62 Luke 4.38–end	Job [12.1] 13 Ephesians 2.1–10	Jeremiah 9.23–24; 10.6–10 Acts 5.17–end *HC Ps 75.1–5; Matt 5.1–12*	*MP* 66 *EP* [67] 68 *DP* 104
Thursday	**5 September** *G*	1 Corinthians 3.18–end Psalm 24.1–6 Luke 5.1–11	Job [12.1] 14 Ephesians 2.11–end	Jeremiah 17.5–14 Acts 6 *HC Ps 1; Matt 5.13–16*	*MP* 69 *EP* 70, 71 *DP* 105
Friday	**6 September** *G* *Allen Gardiner, missionary*	1 Corinthians 4.1–5 Psalm 37.3–8 Luke 5.33–end	Job [16.1] 16.16—end of ch 17 Ephesians 3.1–13	Jeremiah 18.1–17 Acts 7.2–22 *HC Ps 6.1–7; Matt 5.17–20*	*MP* 72 *EP* 73 *DP* 106
Saturday	**7 September** *G*	1 Corinthians 4.6–15 Psalm 145.18–end Luke 6.1–5	Job 19 Ephesians 3.14–end	Jeremiah 20.7–10, 14–end Acts 7.23–50 *HC Ps 55.5–9; Matt 5.21–26*	*MP* 74 *EP* 75, 76 *DP* 107

		Principal Service	3rd Service	2nd Service	Psalmody
Sunday	**8 September** *G* **15th Sunday after Trinity** Proper 18	*Continuous:* Exodus 12.1–14 Psalm 149 *Related:* Ezekiel 33.7–11 Psalm 119.33–40 Romans 13.8–end Matthew 18.15–20	Psalm 119.17–32 Jonah 3.10—4.11 *or* Ecclus 27.30—28.9 Revelation 8.1–5	Psalm 108 [115] Ezekiel 12.21—13.16 Acts 19.1–20 *HC Mark 7.24–end*	*DP* 108

		Holy Communion	Office	2nd Office or Alt HC	Psalmody
Monday	**9 September** *G* *Charles Fuge Lowder, priest* DEL week 23	1 Corinthians 5.1–8 Psalm 5.5–9*a* Luke 6.6–11	Job 22.1—23.7 Ephesians 4.1–16	Jeremiah 22.1–9 Acts 7.51—8.1*a* *HC Ps 41.1–4; Matt 5.27–37*	*MP* 77 *EP* 78.1–20 *DP* 119.153–160
Tuesday	**10 September** *G*	1 Corinthians 6.1–11 Psalm 149.1–5 Luke 6.12–19	Job 29.1–20 Ephesians 4.17–end	Jeremiah 22.13–19 Acts 8.1*b*–25 *HC Ps 101; Matt 5.38–end*	*MP* 78.21–55 *EP* 78.56–end *DP* 109* [*or* 23]
Wednesday	**11 September** *G*	1 Corinthians 7.25–31 Psalm 45.11–end Luke 6.20–26	Job [29.1] 30 Ephesians 5.1–14	Jeremiah 23.1–8 Acts 8.26–end *HC Ps 80.1–8; Matt 6.1–6, 16–18*	*MP* 79 *EP* 80 *DP* 110
Thursday	**12 September** *G*	1 Corinthians 8.1–7, 11–end Psalm 139.1–9 Luke 6.27–38	Job [29.1] 31 Ephesians 5.15–33	Jeremiah 26.1–16 Acts 9.1–19*a* *HC Ps 119.161–168; Matt 6.7–15*	*MP* 81 *EP* 82, 83 *DP* 111
Friday	**13 September** *Gw* John Chrysostom, bishop, teacher of the faith (*see* p.66)	1 Corinthians 9.16–19, 22–end Psalm 84.1–6 Luke 6.39–42	Job 32.1–10 [32.11—33.12*a*]; 33.12*b*–28 Ephesians 6.1–9 *or:* 1st EP of Holy Cross Day: Psalm 66; Isaiah 52.13—end of 53; Ephesians 2.11–end	Jeremiah 28 Acts 9.19*b*–31 *HC Ps 137.1–6; Matt 6.19–24*	*MP* 84 *EP* [85] 86 *DP* 112

		Principal Service	3rd Service	2nd Service	Psalmody
Saturday	**14 September** *R* Holy Cross Day	Numbers 21.4–9 Psalm 22.23–28 Philippians 2.6–11 John 3.13–17	Genesis 3.1–15 John 12.27–36*a*	Isaiah 63.1–16 1 Corinthians 1.18–25	*MP* 2, 8, 146 *EP* 110, 150 *DP* 110

*See page 4, under Psalms.

		Principal Service		3rd Service	2nd Service	Psalmody
Sunday	**15 September** *G* **16th Sunday after Trinity** Proper 19	*Continuous:* Exodus 14.19–end Psalm 114 *or Canticle:* Exodus 15.1*b*–11, 20–21	*Related:* Genesis 50.15–21 Psalm 103.[1–7] 8–13	Psalm 119.65–88 Isaiah 44.24—45.8 Revelation 12.1–12	Psalm 119.41–48 [49–64] Ezekiel 20.1–8, 33–44 Acts 20.17–end *HC Mark 8.27–end*	*DP* 114
		Romans 14.1–12 Matthew 18.21–35				

		Holy Communion	Office	2nd Office or Alt HC	Psalmody
Monday	**16 September** *Gw* Ninian, bishop, missionary (see p.67) *Edward Bouverie Pusey, priest* DEL week 24	1 Corinthians 11.17–26, 33 Psalm 40.7–11 Luke 7.1–10	Job 40 Mark 1.1–13	Jeremiah 31.10–17, 23–25 Acts 10.1–23*a* *HC Ps 149.1–4; Matt 7.1–12*	*MP* 89.19–37 *EP* 89.38–end *DP* 119.161–168
Tuesday	**17 September** *Gw* Hildegard, abbess, visionary (see p.67)	1 Corinthians 12.12–14, 27–end Psalm 100 Luke 7.11–17	Job [40.1] 41.1–11 Mark 1.14–28	Jeremiah 31.27–34 Acts 10.23*b*–end *HC Ps 40.5–9; Matt 7.13–21*	*MP* 90 *EP* [91] 92 *DP* 115
Wednesday	**18 September** *G*	1 Corinthians 12.31*b*—end of 13 Psalm 33.1–12 Luke 7.31–35	Job 42 Mark 1.29–end	Jeremiah 36.1–20 Acts 11.1–18 *HC Ps 7.1–5; Matt 7.22–end*	*MP* 93, 94 *EP* [96] 97 *DP* 116, 117
Thursday	**19 September** *G* *Theodore of Tarsus, archbishop*	1 Corinthians 15.1–11 Psalm 118.1–2, 17–20 Luke 7.36–end	Job 28 Mark 2.1–12	Jeremiah 36.21–31 Acts 11.19–end *HC Ps 52.1–5; Matt 8.1–17*	*MP* [95] 98 *EP* 99 *DP* 118
Friday	**20 September** *Gr* John Coleridge Patteson, bishop, and companions, martyrs (see p.65)	1 Corinthians 15.12–20 Psalm 17.1–8 Luke 8.1–3	Esther 1 *or* Judith 4 Mark 2.13–22	Jeremiah 38.1–13 Acts 12.1–19*a* *HC Ps 142; Matt 8.18–27*	*MP* [100] 101 *EP* 102 *DP* 120
			or: 1st EP of Matthew, apostle and evangelist: Psalm 34; Isaiah 33.13–17; Matthew 6.19–end		

		Principal Service	3rd Service	2nd Service	Psalmody
Saturday	**21 September** *R* Matthew, Apostle and Evangelist	Proverbs 3.13–18 Psalm 119.65–72 2 Corinthians 4.1–6 Matthew 9.9–13	1 Kings 19.15–end 2 Timothy 3.14–end	Ecclesiastes 5.4–12 Matthew 19.16–end	*MP* 49, 117 *EP* 119.33–40, 89–96 *DP* 119.33–40, 89–96

		Principal Service		3rd Service	2nd Service	Psalmody
Sunday	**22 September** *G* **17th Sunday after Trinity** Proper 20	*Continuous:* Exodus 16.2–15 Psalm 105.1–6, 37–end [*or* 105.37–end]	*Related:* Jonah 3.10—end of 4 Psalm 145.1–8	Psalm 119.153–end Isaiah 45.9–22 Revelation 14.1–5	Psalm 119.113–136 [*or* vv 121–128] Ezekiel 33.23, 30—34.10 Acts 26.1, 9–25 *HC Mark 9.30–37*	*DP* 122
		Philippians 1.21–end Matthew 20.1–16				

		Holy Communion	Office	2nd Office or Alt HC	Psalmody
Monday	**23 September** *G* DEL week 25	Proverbs 3.27–34 Psalm 15 Luke 8.16–18	Esther 3.1—4.3 *or* Judith 6.10—7.7, 19–end Mark 3.7–19*a*	1 Samuel 1.1–20 Acts 13.1–12 *HC Ps 5.4–7; Matt 9.1–8*	*MP* 106.1–23 *EP* 106.24–end *DP* 119.169–end
Tuesday	**24 September** *G*	Proverbs 21.1–6, 10–13 Psalm 119.1–8 Luke 8.19–21	Esther 4.4–end *or* Judith 8.9–17; 9.1–10 Mark 3.19*b*–end	1 Samuel 1.21–28 Acts 13.13–31 *HC Ps 48.9–end; Matt 9.9–17*	*MP* 107.1–22 *EP* 107.23–end *DP* 123
Wednesday	**25 September** *Gw* Lancelot Andrewes, bishop, spiritual writer (*see* p.66); Ember Day (see p.6) *Sergei of Radonezh, monk, teacher of the faith*	Proverbs 30.5–9 Psalm 119.105–112 Luke 9.1–6	Esther 5 *or* Judith 10 Mark 4.1–20	1 Samuel 2.1–10 Acts 13.32–43 *HC Ps 113.5–end; Matt 9.18–26*	*MP* 108 [109] *EP* 110, 111 *DP* 124
Thursday	**26 September** *G* *Wilson Carlile*	Ecclesiastes 1.2–11 Psalm 90.1–6 Luke 9.7–9	Esther 6.1–13 *or* Judith 12 Mark 4.21–34	1 Samuel 3 Acts 13.44–end *HC Ps 119.97–100; Matt 9.27–34*	*MP* 112 *EP* 113 *DP* 125
Friday	**27 September** *Gw* Vincent de Paul (see p.67) Ember Day	Ecclesiastes 3.1–11 Psalm 144.1–4 Luke 9.18–22	Esther 6.14—end of 7 *or* Judith 13 Mark 4.35–end	1 Samuel 9.15—10.1; 6–8 Acts 14.1–18 *HC Ps 99.5–7; Matt 9.35—10.4*	*MP* 114 *EP* 115 *DP* 126
Saturday	**28 September** *G* Ember Day	Ecclesiastes 11.9—12.8 Psalm 90.1–2, 12–end Luke 9.43–45	Esther 8; 9.24–28 *or* Judith 15.14—end of ch 16 Mark 5.1–20	1 Samuel 11.12—12.6 Acts 14.19–28 *HC Ps 101.1–6; Matt 10.5–15*	*MP* 116, 117 *EP* 118 *DP* 127
			or, if Michael and All Angels is celebrated on Sunday 29 September: 1st EP of Michael and All Angels: Psalm 91; 2 Kings 6.8–17; Matthew 18.1–6, 10		

Michael and All Angels / Trinity 18

If Michael and All Angels is celebrated on Sunday 29 September:

		Principal Service	3rd Service	2nd Service	Psalmody
Sunday	**29 September** *W* Michael and All Angels	Genesis 28.10–17 *or* Rev 12.7–12 Psalm 103.19–end Rev 12.7–12 *or* Hebrews 1.5–end John 1.47–end	Tobit 12.6–end *or* Daniel 12.1–4 Acts 12.1–11	Daniel 10.4–end Revelation 5	*MP* 34, 150 *EP* 138, 148 *DP* 138
		Holy Communion	**Office**	**2nd Office or Alt HC**	**Psalmody / Alt Pss**
Monday	**30 September** *G* *Jerome, translator of the Scriptures, teacher of the faith* DEL week 26	Job 1.6–end Psalm 17.1–11 Luke 9.46–50	Hosea 1.1—2.1 Mark 5.21–end	1 Samuel 15.10–28 Acts 15.1–21 *HC Ps 50.16–22; Matt 10.16–23*	*MP* 119.1–16 / 23 *EP* 119.17–32 / 25 *DP* 119.1–8

If Michael and All Angels is celebrated on Monday 30 September:

		Principal Service		3rd Service	2nd Service	Psalmody
Sunday	**29 September** *G* **18th Sunday after Trinity** Proper 21	*Continuous:* Exodus 17.1–7 Psalm 78.1–4, 12–16 [*or* 78.1–7] Philippians 2.1–13 Matthew 21.23–32	*Related:* Ezekiel 18.1–4, 25–end Psalm 25.1–8	Psalms 125, 126, 127 Isaiah 48.12–21 Luke 11.37–54	Psalms [120, 123] 124 Ezekiel 37.15–end 1 John 2.22–end *HC Mark 9.38–end* *or:* 1st EP of Michael and All Angels: Psalm 91; 2 Kings 6.8–17; Matthew 18.1–6, 10	*DP* 128

		Holy Communion	Office	2nd Office or Alt HC	Psalmody
Monday	**30 September** *W* Michael and All Angels *(if transferred from 29 September)* *Jerome, translator of the Scriptures, teacher of the faith*	Genesis 28.10–17 *or* Rev 12.7–12 Psalm 103.19–end Rev 12.7–12 *or* Hebrews 1.5–end	Tobit 12.6–end *or* Daniel 12.1–4 Acts 12.1–11 John 1.47–end	Daniel 10.4–end Revelation 5	*MP* 34, 150 *EP* 138, 148 *DP* 138

			Holy Communion	Office	2nd Office or Alt HC	Psalmody	Alt Pss
Tuesday	**1 October** *Remigius, bishop; Anthony Ashley Cooper, Earl of Shaftesbury, social reformer* DEL week 26	*G*	Job 3.1–3, 11–17, 20–23 Psalm 88.14–19 Luke 9.51–56	Hosea 2.2–end Mark 6.1–13	1 Samuel 16.1–13 Acts 15.22–35 *HC Ps 78.69–72; Matt 10.24–33*	*MP* 119.33–48 *EP* 119.49–64 *DP* 129	26 27
Wednesday	**2 October**	*G*	Job 9.1–12, 14–16 Psalm 88.1–6, 11 Luke 9.57–end	Hosea 3.1—4.10 Mark 6.14–29	1 Samuel 17.1–16, 25–50 Acts 15.36—16.10 *HC Ps 92.9–11; Matt 10.34–end*	*MP* 119.65–80 *EP* 119.81–96 *DP* 130	28 29
Thursday	**3 October**	*G*	Job 19.21–27*a* Psalm 27.13–16 Luke 10.1–12	Hosea 4.11–end Mark 6.30–46	1 Samuel 17.58—18.16 Acts 16.11–24 *HC Ps 62.1–5; Matt 11.1–6*	*MP* 119.97–112 *EP* 119.113–128 *DP* 131	30 31
Friday	**4 October** Francis of Assisi, friar, deacon (see p.67)	*Gw*	Job 38.1, 12–21; 40.3–5 Psalm 139.6–11 Luke 10.13–16	Hosea 5.1–7 Mark 6.47–end	1 Samuel 24 Acts 16.25–end *HC Ps 69.1–7; Matt 11.7–15*	*MP* 119.129–144 *EP* 119.145–160 *DP* 132	32 71
Saturday	**5 October**	*G*	Job 42.1–3, 6, 12–end Psalm 119.169–end Luke 10. 17–24	Hosea 5.8—6.11*a* Mark 7.1–23	2 Samuel 1.1–16 Acts 17.1–15 *HC Ps 109.25–end; Matt 11.16–24*	*MP* 119.161–end *EP* 120, 121 *DP* 133	72

		Principal Service		3rd Service	2nd Service	Psalmody
Sunday	**6 October** *G* **19th Sunday after Trinity** Proper 22	*Continuous:* Exodus 20.1–4, 7–9, 12–20 Psalm 19 [*or* 19.7–14]	*Related:* Isaiah 5.1–7 Psalm 80.9–17	Psalms 128, 129, 134 Isaiah 49.13–23 Luke 12.1–12	Psalm 136 [*or* 136.1–9] Proverbs 2.1–11 1 John 2.1–17 *HC Mark 10.2–16*	*DP* 134
		Philippians 3.4*b*–14 Matthew 21.33–end				

Or, when the date of dedication of a church is not known, the Dedication Festival *may be celebrated today or on 27 October, or on a suitable date chosen locally. (See page 65.)*

		Holy Communion	Office	2nd Office or Alt HC	Psalmody
Monday	**7 October** *G* DEL week 27	Galatians 1.6–12 Psalm 111.1–6 Luke 10.25–37	Hosea 6.11*b*—end of 7 Mark 7.24–37	2 Samuel 1.17–end Acts 17.16–end *HC Ps 90.13–end; Matt 11.25–end*	*MP* 122, 123 *EP* 125, 126 *DP* 119.9–16
Tuesday	**8 October** *G*	Galatians 1.13–end Psalm 139.1–9 Luke 10.38–end	Hosea 8 Mark 8.1–10	2 Samuel 2.1–7 Acts 18.1–17 *HC Ps 71.20–end; Matt 12.1–14*	*MP* 126, 127 *EP* 128, 129 *DP* 135
Wednesday	**9 October** *G* *Denys, bishop, and companions, martyrs;* *Robert Grosseteste, bishop*	Galatians 2.1–2, 7–14 Psalm 117 Luke 11.1–4	Hosea 9 Mark 8.11–21	2 Samuel 5.1–5 Acts 18.18–end *HC Ps 89.1–4; Matt 12.15–21*	*MP* 130, 131, 146 *EP* 132 *DP* 136
Thursday	**10 October** *Gw* Paulinus, bishop, missionary (see p.67) *Thomas Traherne, poet, spiritual writer*	Galatians 3.1–5 *Canticle:* Benedictus Luke 11.5–13	Hosea 10 Mark 8.22–33	2 Samuel 5.6–16 Acts 19.1–22 *HC Ps 89.19–24; Matt 12.22–37*	*MP* 133 [134] 147.1–12 *EP* 135 *DP* 137
Friday	**11 October** *G* *Ethelburga, abbess; James the deacon*	Galatians 3.7–14 Psalm 111.4–end Luke 11.15–26	Hosea 11.1—12.6 Mark 8.34—9.1	2 Samuel 6.1–9 Acts 19.23–end *HC Ps 150; Matt 12.38–end*	*MP* 136, 147.13–end *EP* 137, 138 *DP* 138
Saturday	**12 October** *Gw* Wilfrid, bishop, missionary (see p.67) *Elizabeth Fry, prison reformer;* *Edith Cavell, nurse*	Galatians 3.22–end Psalm 105.1–7 Luke 11.27–28	Hosea 12.7—13.3 Mark 9.2–13	2 Samuel 7.1–17 Acts 20.1–12 *HC Ps 132.14–end; Matt 13.1–9*	*MP* 139, 148 *EP* 145 *DP* 139

		Principal Service	3rd Service	2nd Service	Psalmody
Sunday	**13 October** *G* **20th Sunday after Trinity** Proper 23	*Continuous:* Exodus 32.1–14 Psalm 106.1–6, 19–23 [*or* 106.1–6] *Related:* Isaiah 25.1–9 Psalm 23 Philippians 4.1–9 Matthew 22.1–14	Psalms 138, 141 Isaiah 50.4–10 Luke 13.22–30	Psalm 139.1–18 [*or* 1–11] Proverbs 3.1–18 1 John 3.1–15 *HC Mark 10.17–31*	*DP* 140

		Holy Communion	Office	2nd Office or Alt HC	Psalmody
Monday	**14 October** *G* DEL week 28	Galatians 4.21–24, 26–27, 31; 5.1 Psalm 113 Luke 11.29–32	Hosea 13.4—end of 14 Mark 9.14–29	2 Samuel 7.18–end Acts 20.13–end *HC Ps 68.1–4; Matt 13.10–17*	*MP* 141, 149 *EP* 142, 143 *DP* 119.17–24
Tuesday	**15 October** *Gw* Teresa of Avila, teacher of the faith (see p.66)	Galatians 5.1–6 Psalm 119.41–48 Luke 11.37–41	Jonah 1.1–17*a* Mark 9.30–41	2 Samuel 9 Acts 21.1–16 *HC Ps 103.6–12; Matt 13.18–23*	*MP* 144, 150 *EP* 145 *DP* 141
Wednesday	**16 October** *G* *Nicholas Ridley and Hugh Latimer, bishops, martyrs*	Galatians 5.18–end Psalm 1 Luke 11.42–46	Jonah 1.17—end of 2 Mark 9.42–50	2 Samuel 11.1–5, 14–17, 26–end Acts 21.17–36 *HC Ps 125; Matt 13.24–30*	*MP* 1, 2 *EP* 3 [4] *DP* 142
Thursday	**17 October** *Gr* Ignatius, bishop, martyr (see p.65)	Ephesians 1.1, 3–10 Psalm 98.1–4 Luke 11.47–end	Jonah 3.1—end of 4 Mark 10.1–16	2 Samuel 12.1–8*a*; 13 Acts 21.37—22.13 *HC Ps 51.11–15; Matt 13.31–43*	*MP* 5 *EP* 6 *DP* 143
			or: 1st EP of Luke the Evangelist: Psalm 33; Hosea 6.1–3; 2 Timothy 3.10–end		

		Principal Service	3rd Service	2nd Service	Psalmody
Friday	**18 October** *R* Luke the Evangelist	Isaiah 35.3–6 *or* Acts 16.6–12*a* Psalm 147.1–7 2 Timothy 4.5–17 Luke 10.1–9	Isaiah 55 Luke 1.1–4	Ecclesiasticus 38.1–14 *or* Isaiah 61.1–6 Colossians 4.7–end	*MP* 145, 146 *EP* 103 *DP* 103

		Holy Communion	Office	2nd Office or Alt HC	Psalmody
Saturday	**19 October** *Gw* Henry Martyn, translator, missionary (see p.67)	Ephesians 1.15–end Psalm 8 Luke 12.8–12	Ecclesiasticus 3.17–end *or* Micah 2 Mark 10.32–45	2 Samuel 22.1–37, 47–end Acts 22.30—23.11 *HC Ps 31.1–5; Matt 13.53–end*	*MP* 10 *EP* 11, 12 *DP* 145

Trinity 21

		Principal Service	3rd Service	2nd Service	Psalmody
Sunday	**20 October** *G* **21st Sunday after Trinity** Proper 24	*Continuous:* Exodus 33.12–end Psalm 99 *Related:* Isaiah 45.1–7 Psalm 96.1–9 [10–13] 1 Thessalonians 1 Matthew 22.15–22	Psalms 145, 149 Isaiah 54.1–14 Luke 13.31–end	Psalms 142 [143.1–11] Proverbs 4.1–18 1 John 3.16—4.6 *HC Mark 10.35–45*	*DP* 146

		Holy Communion	Office	2nd Office or Alt HC	Psalmody
Monday	**21 October** *G* DEL week 29	Ephesians 2.1–10 Psalm 100 Luke 12.13–21	Ecclesiasticus 4.20—5.7 *or* Micah 3.1–8 Mark 10.46–end	2 Samuel 23.1–7 Acts 23.12–22 *HC Ps 1; Matt 14.1–12*	*MP* 13, 14 *EP* 15, 16 *DP* 119.25–32
Tuesday	**22 October** *G*	Ephesians 2.12–end Psalm 85.7–end Luke 12.35–38	Ecclesiasticus 6.5–17 *or* Micah 3.9—4.5 Mark 11.1–11	2 Samuel 24.18–end Acts 23.23–35 *HC Ps 21.1–7; Matt 14.13–21*	*MP* 19 *EP* 17 *DP* 147
Wednesday	**23 October** *G*	Ephesians 3.2–12 Psalm 98 Luke 12.39–48	Ecclesiasticus 7.4–14 *or* Micah 5.10—6.8 Mark 11.12–26	Amos 2.6–end Acts 24 *HC Ps 38.1–4; Matt 14.22–end*	*MP* 18.1–25 *EP* 18.26–end *DP* 148
Thursday	**24 October** *G*	Ephesians 3.14–end Psalm 33.1–6 Luke 12.49–53	Ecclesiasticus 10.1–18 *or* Micah 7.1–7 Mark 11.27—12.12	Amos 3.1–8 Acts 25.1–12 *HC Ps 119.25–28; Matt 15.1–20*	*MP* 20 *EP* 21 *DP* 149
Friday	**25 October** *G* *Crispin and Crispinian, martyrs*	Ephesians 4.1–6 Psalm 24.1–6 Luke 12.54–end	Ecclesiasticus 11.2–20 *or* Daniel 7.1–14 Mark 12.13–27	Amos 4.1–12 Acts 25.13–end *HC Ps 119.29–31; Matt 15.21–28*	*MP* 22 *EP* 23 [24] *DP* 150
Saturday	**26 October** *Gw* Alfred the Great, king (see p.68) *Cedd, abbot, bishop*	Ephesians 4.7–16 Psalm 122 Luke 13.1–9	Ecclesiasticus 15.9–end *or* Daniel 7.15–end Mark 12.28–end	Amos 5.18–end Acts 26.1–18 *HC Ps 119.153–156; Matt 15.29–end*	*MP* 25 *EP* 26, 27 *DP* 1

		Principal Service		3rd Service	2nd Service	Psalmody
Sunday	**27 October** *G* **Last Sunday after Trinity** Proper 25	*Continuous:* Deuteronomy 34 Psalm 90.1–6, 13–end [*or* 90.1–6] 1 Thessalonians 2.1–8 Matthew 22.34–end	*Related:* Leviticus 19.1–2, 15–18 Psalm 1	Psalm 119.137–152 Isaiah 59.9–20 Luke 14.1–14	Psalm 119.89–104 Ecclesiastes 11, 12 2 Timothy 2.1–7 *HC Mark 12.28–34*	*DP* 2

Or, when the date of dedication of a church is not known, the Dedication Festival *may be celebrated today or on 6 October, or on a suitable date chosen locally. (See page 65.)*

Or, if the Last Sunday after Trinity is being observed as **Bible Sunday**:

		Principal Service	3rd Service	2nd Service	Psalmody
Sunday	**27 October** *G* **Bible Sunday**	Nehemiah 8.1–4*a* [5–6] 8–12 Psalm 119.9–16 Colossians 3.12–17 Matthew 24.30–35	Psalm 119.137–152 Deuteronomy 17.14–15, 18–end John 5.36*b*–end	Psalm 119.89–104 Isaiah 55.1–11 Luke 4.14–30	*DP* 119.1–16
			or: 1st EP of Simon and Jude: Psalms 124, 125, 126; Deuteronomy 32.1–4; John 14.15–26		
Monday	**28 October** *R* Simon and Jude, Apostles	Isaiah 28.14–16 Psalm 119.89–96 Ephesians 2.19–end John 15.17–27	Wisdom 5.1–16 *or* Isaiah 45.18–end Luke 6.12–16	1 Maccabees 2.42–66 *or* Jeremiah 3.11–18 Jude vv 1–4, 17–end	*MP* 116, 117 *EP* 119.1–16 *DP* 119.1–16

		Holy Communion	Office	2nd Office or Alt HC	Psalmody
Tuesday	**29 October** *Gr* James Hannington, bishop, martyr (see p.65) DEL week 30	Ephesians 5.21–end Psalm 128 Luke 13.18–21	Ecclesiasticus 24.1–12 *or* Daniel 8.15–end Mark 13.14–27	Hosea 4.1–9 Acts 27.1–12 *HC Ps 50.1–6; Matt 16.13–end*	*MP* 31.[1–6] 7–end *EP* 32 *DP* 3
Wednesday	**30 October** *G*	Ephesians 6.1–9 Psalm 145.10–20 Luke 13.22–30	Ecclesiasticus 28.14–end *or* Daniel 9.1–9 Mark 13.28—14.2	Hosea 6.1–6 Acts 27.13–26 *HC Ps 50.7–11; Matt 17.1–13*	*MP* 33 *EP* 34 *DP* 4

		Holy Communion	Office	2nd Office or Alt HC	Psalmody
Thursday	**31 October** *G* *Martin Luther, reformer*	Ephesians 6.10–20 Psalm 144.1–2, 9–11 Luke 13.31–end	Ecclesiasticus 31.12—32.2 *or* Daniel 9.20–end Mark 14.3–21	Hosea 11.1–9 Acts 27.27–end *HC Ps 103.6–12; Matt 17.14–21*	*MP* 35 *EP* 36 *DP* 5

All Saints' Day and All Saints' Sunday may both be celebrated, or either may be celebrated.

1st EP of All Saints' Day:
Psalms 1, 5; Ecclus 44.1–15 *or* Isaiah 40.27–end; Revelation 19.6–10

		Principal Service	3rd Service	2nd Service	Psalmody
	Where All Saints' Day is celebrated on Friday 1 November only:				
Friday	**1 November** *W* All Saints' Day	Revelation 7.9–end Psalm 34.1–10 1 John 3.1–3 Matthew 5.1–12	Isaiah 35.1–9 Luke 9.18–27	Isaiah 65.17–end Hebrews 11.32—12.2	*MP* 15, 84, 149 *EP* 148, 150 *DP* 149
	Where All Saints' Day is celebrated on Friday 1 November in addition to All Saints' Sunday on 3 November:				
Or: **Friday**	**1 November** *W* All Saints' Day	Isaiah 56.3–8 *or* 2 Esdras 2.42–end Psalm 33.1–5 Hebrews 12.18–24 Matthew 5.1–12	Wisdom 5.1–16 *or* Jeremiah 31.31–34 2 Corinthians 4.5–12	Isaiah 66.20–23 Colossians 1.9–14	*MP* 111, 112, 117 *EP* 145 *DP* 145

Where All Saints' Day is celebrated on Sunday 3 November only, the following provision should be used on 1 November:

		Holy Communion	Office	2nd Office or Alt HC	Psalmody
Or: **Friday**	**1 November** *G*	Philippians 1.1–11 Psalm 111 Luke 14.1–6	Ecclesiasticus 34.1–22 *or* Daniel 10.1—11.1 Mark 14.22–31	Joel 2.1–14 Acts 28.1–16 *HC Ps 88.9–15; Matt 17.22–end*	*MP* 37.1–22 *EP* 37.23–end *DP* 6
Saturday	**2 November** *R/Gp* Commemoration of the Faithful Departed (All Souls' Day)	Philippians 1.18–26 Psalm 42.1–7 Luke 14.1, 7–11	Ecclesiasticus 35.1–17 *or* Daniel 12† Mark 14.32–52	Joel 2.18–end Acts 28.17–end *HC Ps 4.4–end; Matt 18.1–9*	*MP* 38 *EP* 84 *or* 39 *DP* 7

†*Susanna, and Bel and the Dragon, may be read after Daniel 12.13*

Lesser festival eucharistic lectionary: Lamentations 3.17–26, 31–33 *or* Wisdom 3.1–9; Ps 23 *or* 27.1–6, 16–17; Romans 5.5–11 *or* 1 Peter 1.3–9; John 5.19–25 *or* 6.37–40

1st EP *if* **All Saints' Day** *has not been celebrated on 1 November:*
Psalms 1, 5; Ecclus 44.1–15 *or* Isaiah 40.27–end; Revelation 19.6–10

		Principal Service	3rd Service	2nd Service	Psalmody
Sunday	**3 November** *R/G* **4th Sunday before Advent**	Micah 3.5–end Psalm 43 [*or* 107.1–8] 1 Thessalonians 2.9–13 Matthew 24.1–14	Psalm 33 Isaiah 66.20–23 Ephesians 1.11–end	Psalms 111, 117 Daniel 7.1–18 Luke 6.17–31	*DP* 8

Or, if All Saints' Sunday is being celebrated:

		Principal Service	3rd Service	2nd Service	Psalmody
Sunday	**3 November** *W* **All Saints' Sunday**	Revelation 7.9–end Psalm 34.1–10 1 John 3.1–3 Matthew 5.1–12	Isaiah 35.1–9 Luke 9.18–27	Isaiah 65.17–end Hebrews 11.32—12.2	*MP* 15, 84, 149 *EP* 148, 150 *DP* 149

		Holy Communion	Office	2nd Office or Alt HC	Psalmody	Alt Pss
Monday	**4 November** *R/G* DEL week 31	Philippians 2.1–4 Psalm 131 Luke 14.12–14	Ecclesiasticus 38.24–end *or* 1 Chronicles 17.1–15 Mark 14.53–65	Ezekiel 1.1, 4–13, 22–28*b* Hebrews 1 *HC Ps 97.6–9; Matt 18.10–20*	*MP* 139, 150 *EP* 15, 16 *DP* 119.41–48	40 41
Tuesday	**5 November** *R/G*	Philippians 2.5–11 Psalm 22.22–27 Luke 14.15–24	Ecclesiasticus 43.1–22 *or* 1 Chronicles 28.1–20 Mark 14.66–end	Ezekiel 2.1–2; 3.4–11 Hebrews 2.5–end *HC Ps 131; Matt 18.21–end*	*MP* 116, 146 *EP* 73 *DP* 9	42, 43 44
Wednesday	**6 November** *R/G* *Leonard, hermit; William Temple, archbishop, teacher of the faith*	Philippians 2.12–18 Psalm 27.1–5 Luke 14.25–33	Ecclesiasticus 43.23–end *or* 1 Chronicles 29.1–20 Mark 15.1–15	Ezekiel 20.39–44 Hebrews 4.12—5.10 *HC Ps 126; Matt 19.1–12*	*MP* 65, 147.13–end *EP* 77 *DP* 10	45 46, 47
Thursday	**7 November** *R/Gw* Willibrord of York, bishop (see p.67)	Philippians 3.3–8 Psalm 105.1–7 Luke 15.1–10	Ecclesiasticus 44.1–15 *or* 2 Chronicles 1.1—2.1 Mark 15.16–32	Ezekiel 33.1–9 Hebrews 6.13–end *HC Ps 125; Matt 19.13–22*	*MP* 145, 148 *EP* 34 *DP* 11	48 49
Friday	**8 November** *R/Gw* Saints and martyrs of England	Philippians 3.17—4.1 Psalm 122 Luke 16.1–8 *Lesser festival eucharistic lectionary:* Isaiah 61.4–9 *or* Ecclesiasticus 44.1–15; Psalm 15; Revelation 19.5–10; John 17.18–23	Ecclesiasticus 50.1–24 *or* 2 Chronicles 5 Mark 15.33–end	Ezekiel 34.1–6 Hebrews 7.11–end *HC Ps 86.12–end; Matt 19.23–end*	*MP* 23, 125, 147.1–12 *EP* 142, 143 *DP* 12	50 51
Saturday	**9 November** *R/G* *Margery Kempe, mystic*	Philippians 4.10–19 Psalm 112 Luke 16.9–15	Ecclesiasticus 51.1–12 *or* 2 Chronicles 6.1–21 Mark 16.1–8 [9–20]	Ezekiel 36.22–36 Hebrews 8.1–12 *HC Ps 87; Matt 20.1–16*	*MP* 92, 97, 149 *EP* 84 *DP* 13	52, 53 54, 55

		Principal Service		3rd Service	2nd Service	Psalmody
Sunday	**10 November** *R/G* **3rd Sunday before Advent** *Remembrance Sunday*	Wisdom 6.12–16 *Canticle:* Wisdom 6.17–20 I Thessalonians 4.13–end Matthew 25.1–13	Amos 5.18–24 Psalm 70	Psalm 91 Deuteronomy 17.14–end I Timothy 2.1–7	Psalms [20] 82 Judges 7.2–22 John 15.9–17	*DP* 14

		Holy Communion	Office	2nd Office or Alt HC	Psalmody	Alt Pss
Monday	**11 November** *R/Gw* Martin of Tours, bishop (see p.67) DEL week 32	Titus 1.1–9 Psalm 24.1–6 Luke 17.1–6	Joel 1.1–13 2 Corinthians 1.1–11	Ezekiel 37.1–14 Hebrews 9.11–end *HC Ps 119.169–end; Matt 20.17–28*	*MP* 139, 150 *EP* 15, 16 *DP* 119.49–56	56 57
Tuesday	**12 November** *R/G*	Titus 2.1–8, 11–14 Psalm 37.3–5, 30–32 Luke 17.7–10	Joel 1.14—2.2 [3–11] 2 Corinthians 1.12–22	Ezekiel 47.1–12 Hebrews 10.1–18 *HC Ps 103.19–end; Matt 20.29–end*	*EP* 73 *MP* 116, 146 *DP* 15	[58] 59 60
Wednesday	**13 November** *R/Gw* Charles Simeon, priest, evangelical divine (see p.66)	Titus 3.1–7 Psalm 23 Luke 17.11–19	Joel 2.12–19 2 Corinthians 1.23—end of 2	Zephaniah 1.1–9 Hebrews 10.19–25, 35–end *HC Ps 44.21–end; Matt 21.1–9*	*MP* 65, 147.13–end *EP* 77 *DP* 16	61 62
Thursday	**14 November** *R/G* *Samuel Seabury, bishop*	Philemon 7–20 Psalm 146.4–end Luke 17.20–25	Joel 2.21–27 2 Corinthians 3	Zephaniah 3.8–13 Hebrews 11 *HC Ps 22.22–27; Matt 21.10–22*	*MP* 145, 148 *EP* 34 *DP* 17	[63] 64 65
Friday	**15 November** *R/G*	2 John vv 4–9 Psalm 119.1–8 Luke 17.26–end	Joel 2.28—3.8 2 Corinthians 4.1–12	Zephaniah 3.14–end Hebrews 12.1–13 *HC Ps 149.4–end; Matt 21.23–32*	*MP* 23, 125, 147.1–12 *EP* 142, 143 *DP* 18	66 [67] 68
Saturday	**16 November** *R/Gw* Margaret of Scotland (see p.68) *Edmund Rich, bishop*	3 John vv 5–8 Psalm 112 Luke 18.1–8	Joel 3.9–17 2 Corinthians 4.13—5.10	Zechariah 1.1–6 Hebrews 12.14–end *HC Ps 80.15–19; Matt 21.33–end*	*MP* 92, 97, 149 *EP* 84 *DP* 19	69 70, 71

		Principal Service	3rd Service	2nd Service	Psalmody
Sunday	**17 November** *R/G* **2nd Sunday before Advent**	Zephaniah 1.7, 12–end Psalm 90.1–8 [9–11] 12 [*or* 90.1–8] 1 Thessalonians 5.1–11 Matthew 25.14–30	Psalm 98 Daniel 10.19–end Revelation 4	Psalm 89.19–37 [*or* 89.19–29] 1 Kings 1.15–40 [*or* 1–40] Revelation 1.4–18 *HC Luke 9.1–6*	*DP* 20

		Holy Communion	Office	2nd Office or Alt HC	Psalmody	Alt Pss
Monday	**18 November** *R/Gw* Elizabeth of Hungary (see p.68) DEL week 33	Revelation 1.1–4; 2.1–5 Psalm 1 Luke 18.35–end	Habakkuk 2 2 Corinthians 5.11—6.2	Zechariah 2.1–5 Hebrews 13 *HC Ps 27.1–5; Matt 22.1–14*	*MP* 139, 150 *EP* 15, 16 *DP* 119.57–64	72 73
Tuesday	**19 November** *R/Gw* Hilda, abbess (see p.67) *Mechtild, mystic*	Revelation 3.1–6, 14–end Psalm 15 Luke 19.1–10	Habakkuk 3.1–18 2 Corinthians 6.3—7.1	Zechariah 4 James 1.16–25 *HC Ps 87; Matt 22.15–22*	*MP* 116, 146 *EP* 73 *DP* 21	74 75, 76
Wednesday	**20 November** *R/Gr* Edmund, king, martyr (see p.65) *Priscilla Lydia Sellon*	Revelation 4 Psalm 150 Luke 19.11–28	Malachi 1.1, 6–end 2 Corinthians 7.2–end	Zechariah 8.1–13 James 2.1–13 *HC Ps 84.1–4; Matt 22.23–33*	*MP* 65, 147.13–end *EP* 77 *DP* 22	77 78.1–20
Thursday	**21 November** *R/G*	Revelation 5.1–10 Psalm 149.1–5 Luke 19.41–44	Malachi 2.1–16 2 Corinthians 8.1–15	Zechariah 9.9–12 James 2.14–24 *HC Ps 72.1–8; Matt 22.34–end*	*MP* 145, 148 *EP* 34 *DP* 23	78.21–55 78.56–end
Friday	**22 November** *R/G* *Cecilia, martyr*	Revelation 10.8–11 Psalm 119.65–72 Luke 19.45–end	Malachi 3.1–12 2 Corinthians 8.16–end	Daniel 1.1–7, 20–end James 4.1–12 *HC Ps 37.1–6; Matt 23.1–12*	*MP* 23, 125, 147.1–12 *EP* 142, 143 *DP* 24	79 80
Saturday	**23 November** *R/Gr* Clement, bishop, martyr (see p.65)	Revelation 11.4–12 Psalm 144.1–9 Luke 20.27–40	Malachi 3.13—end of 4 2 Corinthians 9	Daniel 2.1–5, 24–45 James 5.1–12 *HC Ps 119.161–166; Matt 23.13–26*	*MP* 92, 97, 149 *EP* 99, 100 *DP* 25	81 82, 83
			or: 1st EP of Christ the King: Psalms 99, 100; Isaiah 10.33—11.9; 1 Timothy 6.11–16			

		Principal Service	3rd Service	2nd Service	Psalmody
Sunday	**24 November** *W* Christ the King *Sunday next before Advent*	Ezekiel 34.11–16, 20–24 Psalm 95.1–7 Ephesians 1.15–end Matthew 25.31–end	Isaiah 4.2—5.7 Luke 19.29–38	2 Samuel 23.1–7 *or* 1 Maccabees 2.15–29 Matthew 28.16–end	*MP* 29, 110 *EP* 93 [97] *DP* 26

		Holy Communion	Office	2nd Office or Alt HC	Psalmody	Alt Pss
Monday	**25 November** *R/G* *Catherine of Alexandria, martyr; Isaac Watts, hymn writer* DEL week 34	Revelation 14.1–5 Psalm 24.1–6 Luke 21.1–4	Zechariah 10 2 Corinthians 10	Daniel 3.1–12 James 5.13–end *HC Ps 37.7–11; Matt 23.29– end*	*MP* 139, 150 *EP* 15, 16 *DP* 119.65–72	84 [85] 86
Tuesday	**26 November** *R/G*	Revelation 14.14–19 Psalm 96 Luke 21.5–11	Zechariah 11.4–end 2 Corinthians 11.1–21*a*	Daniel 3.13–18 1 John 1 *HC Ps 37.12–17; Matt 24.1–14*	*MP* 116, 146 *EP* 73 *DP* 27	87, 88 89.1–18
Wednesday	**27 November** *R/G*	Revelation 15.1–4 Psalm 98 Luke 21.12–19	Zechariah 12.1–10 2 Corinthians 11.21*b*–end	Daniel 5.1–8 1 John 2.1–11 *HC Ps 94.8–11; Matt 24.15–28*	*MP* 65, 147.13–end *EP* 77 *DP* 28	89.19–37 89.38–end
Thursday	**28 November** *R/G*	Revelation 18.1–2, 21–23; 19.1–3, 9 Psalm 100 Luke 21.20–28	Zechariah 13 2 Corinthians 12.1–10	Daniel 5.13–30 1 John 3.11–end *HC Ps 46.8– end; Matt 24.29–36*	*MP* 145, 148 *EP* 34 *DP* 29	90 [91] 92
Friday	**29 November** *R/G* *Day of Intercession and Thanksgiving for the Missionary Work of the Church*	Revelation 20.1–4, 11—21.2 Psalm 84.1–6 Luke 21.29–33	Zechariah 14.1–11 2 Corinthians 12.11–end	Daniel 6.1–23 1 John 4.7–end *HC Ps 54; Matt 24.37–51* *or:* 1st EP of Andrew the Apostle: Psalm 48; Isaiah 49.1–9*a*; 1 Corinthians 4.9–16	*MP* 23, 125, 147.1–12 *EP* 142, 143 *DP* 30	93, 94 [96] 97

		Principal Service	3rd Service	2nd Service	Psalmody
Saturday	**30 November** *R* Andrew the Apostle	Isaiah 52.7–10 Psalm 19.1–6 Romans 10.12–18 Matthew 4.18–22	Ezekiel 47.1–12 *or* Ecclesiasticus 14.20–end John 12.20–32	Zechariah 8.20–end John 1.35–42	*MP* 47, 147.1–12 *EP* 87, 96 *DP* 87

¶ *Lectionary for Dedication Festival*

If date not known, observe on the First Sunday in October or Last Sunday after Trinity.

Evening Prayer on the Eve
Psalm 24
2 Chronicles 7.11-16
John 4.19-29

Principal Service
1 Kings 8.22-30 *or*
Revelation 21.9-14
Psalm 122
Hebrews 12.18-24
Matthew 21.12-16

Second Service
Jeremiah 7.1-11
1 Corinthians 3.9-17
Gospel at Holy Communion:
Luke 19.1-10
Evening Psalm
Psalm 132

Third Service
Haggai 2.6-9
Hebrews 10.19-25
Morning Psalms
Psalms 48, 150

¶ *Lectionary for Common of the Saints*

The Blessed Virgin Mary

Genesis 3.8–15, 20; Isaiah 7.10–14; Micah 5.1–4
Psalms 45.10–17; 113; 131
Acts 1.12–14; Romans 8.18–30; Galatians 4.4–7
Luke 1.26–38; *or* 1.39–47; John 19.25–27

Martyrs

2 Chronicles 24.17–21; Isaiah 43.1–7; Jeremiah 11.18–20; Wisdom 4.10–15
Psalms 3; 11; 31.1–5; 44.18–24; 126
Romans 8.35–end; 2 Corinthians 4.7–15; 2 Timothy 2.3–7 [8–13]; Hebrews 11.32–end; 1 Peter 4.12–end; Revelation 12.10–12*a*
Matthew 10.16–22; *or* 10.28–39; *or* 16.24–26; John 12.24–26; *or* 15.18–21

Agnes (21 Jan): *also* Revelation 7.13–end
Alban (22 June): *especially* 2 Timothy 2.3–13; John 12.24–26
Alphege (19 Apr): *also* Hebrews 5.1–4
Boniface (5 June): *also* Acts 20.24–28
Charles (30 Jan): *also* Ecclesiasticus 2.12–end; 1 Timothy 6.12–16
Clement (23 Nov): *also* Philippians 3.17—4.3; Matthew 16.13–19
Cyprian (15 Sept): *especially* 1 Peter 4.12–end; *also* Matthew 18.18–22
Edmund (20 Nov): *also* Proverbs 20.28; 21.1–4, 7
Ignatius (17 Oct): *also* Philippians 3.7–12; John 6.52–58
James Hannington (29 Oct): *especially* Matthew 10.28–39
Janani Luwum (17 Feb): *also* Ecclesiasticus 4.20–28; John 12.24–32
John Coleridge Patteson (20 Sept): *especially* 2 Chronicles 24.17–21; *also* Acts 7.55–end
Justin (1 June): *especially* John 15.18–21; *also* 1 Maccabees 2.15–22; 1 Corinthians 1.18–25
Laurence (10 Aug): *also* 2 Corinthians 9.6–10
Lucy (13 Dec): *also* Wisdom 3.1–7; 2 Corinthians 4.6–15
Oswald (5 Aug): *especially* 1 Peter 4.12–end; John 16.29–end
Perpetua, Felicity and comps (7 Mar): *especially* Revelation 12.10–12*a*; *also* Wisdom 3.1–7
Polycarp (23 Feb): *also* Revelation 2.8–11
Thomas Becket (29 Dec *or* 7 Jul): *especially* Matthew 10.28–33; *also* Ecclesiasticus 51.1–8
William Tyndale (6 Oct): *also* Proverbs 8.4–11; 2 Timothy 3.12–end

Teachers of the Faith and Spiritual Writers

1 Kings 3.[6–10] 11–14; Proverbs 4.1–9; Wisdom 7.7–10, 15–16; Ecclesiasticus 39.1–10
Psalms 19.7–10; 34.11–17; 37.31–35; 119.89–96; 119.97–104
1 Corinthians 1.18–25; *or* 2.1–10; *or* 2.9–end; Ephesians 3.8–12; 2 Timothy 4.1–8; Titus 2.1–8
Matthew 5.13–19; *or* 13.52–end; *or* 23.8–12; Mark 4.1–9; John 16.12–15

Ambrose (7 Dec): *also* Isaiah 41.9*b*–13; Luke 22.24–30
Anselm (21 Apr): *also* Wisdom 9.13–end; Romans 5.8–11
Athanasius (2 May): *also* Ecclesiasticus 4.20–28; *also* Matthew 10.24–27
Augustine of Hippo (28 Aug): *especially* Ecclesiasticus 39.1–10; *also* Romans 13.11–13
Basil and Gregory (2 Jan): *especially* 2 Timothy 4.1–8; Matthew 5.13–19
Bernard (20 Aug): *especially* Revelation 19.5–9
Catherine of Siena (29 Apr): *also* Proverbs 8.1, 6–11; John 17.12–end
Francis de Sales (24 Jan): *also* Proverbs 3.13–18; John 3.17–21
Gregory the Great (3 Sept): *also* 1 Thessalonians 2.3–8
Gregory of Nyssa and Macrina (19 July): *especially* 1 Corinthians 2.9–13; *also* Wisdom 9.13–17
Hilary (13 Jan): *also* 1 John 2.18–25; John 8.25–32
Irenaeus (28 June): *also* 2 Peter 1.16–end
Jeremy Taylor (13 Aug): *also* Titus 2.7–8, 11–14
John Bunyan (30 Aug): *also* Hebrews 12.1–2; Luke 21.21, 34–36
John Chrysostom (13 Sept): *especially* Matthew 5.13–19; *also* Jeremiah 1.4–10
John of the Cross (14 Dec): *especially* 1 Corinthians 2.1–10; *also* John 14.18–23
Leo (10 Nov): *also* 1 Peter 5.1–11
Richard Hooker (3 Nov): *especially* John 16.12–15; *also* Ecclesiasticus 44.10–15
Teresa of Avila (15 Oct): *also* Romans 8.22–27
Thomas Aquinas (28 Jan): *especially* Wisdom 7.7–10, 15–16; 1 Corinthians 2.9–end; John 16.12–15
William Law (10 Apr): *especially* 1 Corinthians 2.9–end; *also* Matthew 17.1–9

Bishops and Other Pastors

1 Samuel 16.1, 6–13; Isaiah 6.1–8; Jeremiah 1.4–10; Ezekiel 3.16–21; Malachi 2.5–7
Psalms 1; 15; 16.5–end; 96; 110
Acts 20.28–35; 1 Corinthians 4.1–5; 2 Corinthians 4.1–10 [*or* 1–2, 5–7]; *or* 5.14–20; 1 Peter 5.1–4
Matthew 11.25–end; *or* 24.42–46; John 10.11–16; *or* 15.9–17; *or* 21.15–17

Augustine of Canterbury (26 May): *also* 1 Thessalonians 2.2*b*–8; Matthew 13.31–33
Charles Simeon (13 Nov): *especially* Malachi 2.5–7; *also* Colossians 1.3–8; Luke 8.4–8
David (1 Mar): *also* 2 Samuel 23.1–4; Psalm 89.19–22, 24
Dunstan (19 May): *especially* Matthew 24.42–46; *also* Exodus 31.1–5
Edward King (8 Mar): *also* Hebrews 13.1–8
George Herbert (27 Feb): *especially* Malachi 2.5–7; Matthew 11.25–end; *also* Revelation 19.5–9
Hugh (17 Nov): *also* 1 Timothy 6.11–16
John Keble (14 July): *also* Lamentations 3.19–26; Matthew 5.1–8
John and Charles Wesley (24 May): *also* Ephesians 5.15–20
Lancelot Andrewes (25 Sept): *especially* Isaiah 6.1–8

Martin of Tours (11 Nov): *also* 1 Thessalonians 5.1–11; Matthew 25.34–40
Nicholas (6 Dec): *also* Isaiah 61.1–3; 1 Timothy 6.6–11; Mark 10.13–16
Richard (16 June): *also* John 21.15–19
Swithun (15 July): *also* James 5.7–11, 13–18
Thomas Ken (8 June): *especially* 2 Corinthians 4.1–10 [*or* 1–2, 5–7]; Matthew 24.42–46
Wulfstan (19 Jan): *especially* Matthew 24.42–46

Members of Religious Communities

1 Kings 19.9–18; Proverbs 10.27–end; Song of Solomon 8.6–7; Isaiah 61.10—62.5; Hosea 2.14–15, 19–20
Psalms 34.1–8; 112.1–9; 119.57–64; 123; 131
Acts 4.32–35; 2 Corinthians 10.17—11.2; Philippians 3.7–14; 1 John 2.15–17; Revelation 19.1, 5–9
Matthew 11.25–end; *or* 19.3–12; *or* 19.23–end; Luke 9.57–end; *or* 12.32–37

Aelred (12 Jan): *also* Ecclesiasticus 15.1–6
Alcuin (20 May): *also* Colossians 3.12–16; John 4.19–24
Antony (17 Jan): *especially* Philippians 3.7–14, *also* Matthew 19.16–26
Bede (25 May): *also* Ecclesiasticus 39.1–10
Benedict (11 July): *also* 1 Corinthians 3.10–11; Luke 18.18–22
Clare (11 Aug): *especially* Song of Solomon 8.6–7
Dominic (8 Aug): *also* Ecclesiasticus 39.1–10
Etheldreda (23 June): *also* Matthew 25.1–13
Francis of Assisi (4 Oct): *also* Galatians 6.14–end; Luke 12.22–34
Hilda (19 Nov): *especially* Isaiah 61.10—62.5
Hildegard (17 Sept): *also* 1 Corinthians 2.9–13; Luke 10.21–24
Julian of Norwich (8 May): *also* 1 Corinthians 13.8–end; Matthew 5.13–16
Vincent de Paul (27 Sept): *also* 1 Corinthians 1.25–end; Matthew 25.34–40

Missionaries

Isaiah 52.7–10; *or* 61.1–3*a*; Ezekiel 34.11–16; Jonah 3.1–5
Psalms 67; *or* 87; *or* 97; *or* 100; *or* 117
Acts 2.14, 22–36; *or* 13.46–49; *or* 16.6–10; *or* 26.19–23; Romans 15.17–21; 2 Corinthians 5.11—6.2
Matthew 9.35–end; *or* 28.16–end; Mark 16.15–20; Luke 5.1–11; *or* 10.1–9

Aidan (31 Aug): *also* 1 Corinthians 9.16–19
Anskar (3 Feb): *especially* Isaiah 52.7–10; *also* Romans 10.11–15
Chad (2 Mar *or* 26 Oct): *also* 1 Timothy 6.11*b*–16
Columba (9 June): *also* Titus 2.11–end
Cuthbert (20 Mar *or* 4 Sept): *especially* Ezekiel 34.11–16; *also* Matthew 18.12–14
Cyril and Methodius (14 Feb): *especially* Isaiah 52.7–10; *also* Romans 10.11–15
Henry Martyn (19 Oct): *especially* Mark 16.15–end; *also* Isaiah 55.6–11
Ninian (16 Sept): *especially* Acts 13.46–49; Mark 16.15–end
Patrick (17 Mar): *also* Psalm 91.1–4, 13–16; Luke 10.1–12, 17–20
Paulinus (10 Oct): *especially* Matthew 28.16–end
Wilfrid (12 Oct): *especially* Luke 5.1–11; *also* 1 Corinthians 1.18–25
Willibrord (7 Nov): *especially* Isaiah 52.7–10; Matthew 28.16–end

Any Saint

General

Genesis 12.1–4; Proverbs 8.1–11; Micah 6.6–8; Ecclesiasticus 2.7–13 [14–end]
Psalms 32; 33.1–5; 119.1–8; 139.1–4 [5–12]; 145.8–14
Ephesians 3.14–19; *or* 6.11–18; Hebrews 13.7–8, 15–16; James 2.14–17;
1 John 4.7–16; Revelation 21.[1–4] 5–7
Matthew 19.16–21; *or* 25.1–13; *or* 25.14–30; John 15.1–8; *or* 17.20–end

Christian rulers

1 Samuel 16.1–13*a*; 1 Kings 3.3–14
Psalms 72.1–7; 99
1 Timothy 2.1–6
Mark 10.42–45; Luke 14.27–33

Alfred the Great (26 Oct): *also* 2 Samuel 23.1–5; John 18.33–37
Edward the Confessor (13 Oct): *also* 2 Samuel 23.1–5; 1 John 4.13–16
Margaret of Scotland (16 Nov): *also* Proverbs 31.10–12, 20, 26–end;
1 Corinthians 12.13—13.3; Matthew 25.34–end

Those working for the poor and underprivileged

Isaiah 58.6–11
Psalms 82; 146.5–10
Hebrews 13.1–3; 1 John 3.14–18
Matthew 5.1–12; *or* 25.31–end

Elizabeth of Hungary (18 Nov): *especially* Matthew 25.31–end; *also* Proverbs 31.10–end
Josephine Butler (30 May): *especially* Isaiah 58.6–11; *also* 1 John 3.18–23; Matthew 9.10–13
William Wilberforce (30 July): *also* Job 31.16–23; Galatians 3.26–end, 4.6–7; Luke 4.16–21

Men and women of learning

Proverbs 8.22–31; Ecclesiasticus 44.1–15
Psalms 36.5–10; 49.1–4
Philippians 4.7–8
Matthew 13.44–46, 52; John 7.14–18

Those whose holiness was revealed in marriage and family life

Proverbs 31.10–13, 19–20, 30–end; Tobit 8.4–7
Psalms 127; 128
1 Peter 3.1–9
Mark 3.31–35; Luke 10.38–end

Mary Sumner (9 Aug): *also* Hebrews 13.1–5
Monica (27 Aug): *also* Ecclesiasticus 26.1–3, 13–16

The Guidance of the Holy Spirit

Proverbs 24.3–7; Isaiah 30.15–21; Wisdom 9.13–17
Psalms 25.1–9; 104.26–33; 143.8–10
Acts 15.23–29; Romans 8.22–27; 1 Corinthians 12.4–13
Luke 14.27–33; John 14.23–26; *or* 16.13–15

Rogation Days
(6–8 May in 2002)

Deuteronomy 8.1–10; 1 Kings 8.35–40; Job 28.1–11
Psalms 104.21–30; 107.1–9; 121
Philippians 4.4–7; 2 Thessalonians 3.6–13; 1 John 5.12–15
Matthew 6.1–15; Mark 11.22–24; Luke 11.5–13

Harvest Thanksgiving

Year A	Year B	Year C
Deuteronomy 8.7–18 *or* 28.1–14	Joel 2.21–27	Deuteronomy 26.1–11
Psalm 65	Psalm 126	Psalm 100
2 Corinthians 9.6–end	1 Timothy 2.1–7 *or* 6.6–10	Philippians 4.4–9 *or* Revelation 14.14–18
Luke 12.16–30 *or* 17.11–19	Matthew 6.25–33	John 6.25–35

Mission and Evangelism

Isaiah 49.1–6; *or* 52.7–10; Micah 4.1–5
Psalms 2; 46; 67
Acts 17.12–end; 2 Corinthians 5.14—6.2; Ephesians 2.13–end
Matthew 5.13–16; *or* 28.16–end; John 17.20–end

The Unity of the Church

Jeremiah 33.6–9*a*; Ezekiel 36.23–28; Zephaniah 3.16–end
Psalms 100; 122; 133
Ephesians 4.1–6; Colossians 3.9–17; 1 John 4.9–15
Matthew 18.19–22; John 11.45–52; *or* 17.11*b*–23

The Peace of the World

Isaiah 9.1–6; *or* 57.15–19; Micah 4.1–5
Psalms 40.14–17; 72.1–7; 85.8–13
Philippians 4.6–9; 1 Timothy 2.1–6; James 3.13–18
Matthew 5.43–end; John 14.23–29; *or* 15.9–17

Social Justice and Responsibility

Isaiah 32.15–end; Amos 5.21–24; *or* 8.4–7; Acts 5.1–11
Psalms 31.21–24; 85.1–7; 146.5–10
Colossians 3.12–15; James 2.1–4
Matthew 5.1–12; *or* 25.31–end; Luke 16.19–end

Ministry, including Ember Days

(See page 6)

Numbers 11.16–17, 24–29; *or* 27.15–end; 1 Samuel 16.1–13*a*; Isaiah 6.1–8;
or 61.1–3; Jeremiah 1.4–10

Psalms 40.8–13; 84.8–12; 89.19–25; 101.1–5, 7; 122

Acts 20.28–35; 1 Corinthians 3.3–11; Ephesians 4.4–16; Philippians 3.7–14

Luke 4.16–21; *or* 12.35–43; *or* 22.24–27; John 4.31–38; *or* 15.5–17

In Time of Trouble

Genesis 9.8–17; Job 1.13–end; Isaiah 38.6–11

Psalms 86.1–7; 107.4–15; 142.1–7

Romans 3.21–26; Romans 8.18–25; 2 Corinthians 8.1–5, 9

Mark 4.35–end; Luke 12.1–7; John 16.31–end

For the Sovereign

Joshua 1.1–9; Proverbs 8.1–16

Psalms 20; 101; 121

Romans 13.1–10; Revelation 21.22—22.4

Matthew 22.16–22; Luke 22.24–30

The anniversary of HM The Queen's accession is 6 February.

Psalms in the Course of a Month

The following provision may be used for a monthly cycle of psalmody in place of the psalms provided in the tables in this booklet. It is based on the provision in The Book of Common Prayer.

	Morning Prayer	**Evening Prayer**
1	1—5	6—8
2	9—11	12—14
3	15—17	18
4	19—21	22—23
5	24—26	27—29
6	30—31	32—34
7	35—36	37
8	38—40	41—43
9	44—46	47—49
10	50—52	53—55
11	56—58	59—61
12	62—64	65—67
13	68	69—70
14	71—72	73—74
15	75—77	78
16	79—81	82—85
17	86—88	89
18	90—92	93—94
19	95—97	98—101
20	102—103	104
21	105	106
22	107	108—109
23	110—112	113—115
24	116—118	119.1–32
25	119.33–72	119.73–96
26	119.97–144	119.145–176
27	120—125	126—131
28	132—135	136—138
29	139—140	141—143
30	144—146	147—150

In February the psalms are read only to the 28th or 29th day of the month.

In January, March, May, July, August, October and December, all of which have 31 days, the same psalms are read on the last day of the month (being an ordinary weekday) which were read the day before, or else the psalms of the monthly course omitted on one of the Sundays in that month.

Concise Calendar December 2002 – December 2003

Advent 2002 to the eve of Advent 2003: Year B (Weekday Lectionary Year 1)

December 2002					
Sunday	Adv1	Adv2	Adv3	Adv4	Chr1
Monday	2	9	16	23	30
Tuesday	3	10	17	24	31
Wednesday	4	11	18	Chr	
Thursday	5	12	19	26	
Friday	6	13	20	27	
Saturday	7	14	21	28	

January					
Sunday		Chr2	Bapt	Ep2	Ep3
Monday		Ep	13	20	27
Tuesday		7	14	21	28
Wednesday	1	8	15	22	29
Thursday	2	9	16	23	30
Friday	3	10	17	24	31
Saturday	4	11	18	25	

February					
Sunday		Pres	4bLnt	3bLnt	2bLnt
Monday		3	10	17	24
Tuesday		4	11	18	25
Wednesday		5	12	19	26
Thursday		6	13	20	27
Friday		7	14	21	28
Saturday	1	8	15	22	

March						
Sunday		SbLnt	Lnt1	Lnt2	Lnt3	Lnt4
Monday		3	10	17	24	31
Tuesday		4	11	18	Ann	
Wednesday		Ash	12	19	26	
Thursday		6	13	20	27	
Friday		7	14	21	28	
Saturday	1	8	15	22	29	

April					
Sunday		Lnt5	PmS	Est	Est2
Monday		7	14	21	28
Tuesday	1	8	15	22	29
Wednesday	2	9	16	23	30
Thursday	3	10	MTh	24	
Friday	4	11	GFr	25	
Saturday	5	12	19	26	

May					
Sunday		Est3	Est4	Est5	Est6
Monday		5	12	19	26
Tuesday		6	13	20	27
Wednesday		7	14	21	28
Thursday	1	8	15	22	Ascn
Friday	2	9	16	23	30
Saturday	3	10	17	24	31

June					
Sunday	Est7	Pent	TrS	Tr1	Tr2
Monday	2	9	16	23	30
Tuesday	3	10	17	24	
Wednesday	4	11	18	25	
Thursday	5	12	19	26	
Friday	6	13	20	27	
Saturday	7	14	21	28	

July					
Sunday		Tr3	Tr4	Tr5	Tr6
Monday		7	14	21	28
Tuesday	1	8	15	22	29
Wednesday	2	9	16	23	30
Thursday	3	10	17	24	31
Friday	4	11	18	25	
Saturday	5	12	19	26	

August						
Sunday		Tr7	Tr8	Tr9	Tr10	Tr11
Monday		4	11	18	25	
Tuesday		5	12	19	26	
Wednesday		6	13	20	27	
Thursday		7	14	21	28	
Friday	1	8	15	22	29	
Saturday	2	9	16	23	30	

September					
Sunday		Tr12	Tr13	Tr14	Tr15
Monday	1	8	15	22	29
Tuesday	2	9	16	23	30
Wednesday	3	10	17	24	
Thursday	4	11	18	25	
Friday	5	12	19	26	
Saturday	6	13	20	27	

October					
Sunday		Tr16	Tr17	Tr18	Tr19
Monday		6	13	20	27
Tuesday		7	14	21	28
Wednesday	1	8	15	22	29
Thursday	2	9	16	23	30
Friday	3	10	17	24	31
Saturday	4	11	18	25	

November						
Sunday		4bAdv	3bAdv	2bAdv	ChrK	Adv1
Monday		3	10	17	24	
Tuesday		4	11	18	25	
Wednesday		5	12	19	26	
Thursday		6	13	20	27	
Friday		7	14	21	28	
Saturday	All SS	8	15	22	29	

December 2003					
Sunday		Adv2	Adv3	Adv4	Chr1
Monday	1	8	15	22	29
Tuesday	2	9	16	23	30
Wednesday	3	10	17	24	31
Thursday	4	11	18	Chr	
Friday	5	12	19	26	
Saturday	6	13	20	27	

Sunday 5 January may be celebrated as **Epiphany**, transferred from Monday 6th.
Sunday 29 June may be celebrated as Peter and Paul, Apostles.
Sunday 24 August may be celebrated as Bartholomew the Apostle.
Sunday 14 September may be celebrated as Holy Cross Day.
Sunday 21 September may be celebrated as Matthew, Apostle and Evangelist.
Sunday 2 November may be celebrated as **All Saints' Sunday**.
Sunday 28 December 2003 may be celebrated as the Holy Innocents.